REDISCOVER THE JOYS AND BEAUTY OF NATURE WITH TOM BROWN, JR.

THE TRACKER

Tom Brown's classic true story—the most powerful and magical high-spiritual adventure since *The Teachings of Don Juan.*

THE SEARCH

The continuing story of *The Tracker*, exploring the ancient art of the new survival.

THE VISION

Tom Brown's profound, personal journey into an ancient mystical experience, the Vision Quest.

THE QUEST

The acclaimed outdoorsman shows how we can save our planet.

THE JOURNEY

A message of hope and harmony for our earth and our spirits—Tom Brown's vision for healing our world.

GRANDFATHER

The incredible true story of a remarkable Native American and his lifelong search for peace and truth in nature.

AWAKENING SPIRITS

For the first time, Tom Brown shares the unique meditation exercises used by students of his personal Tracker classes.

AND HIS UNIQUE, BESTSELLING WILDERNESS SERIES:

TOM BROWN'S FIELD GUIDE TO NATURE
AND SURVIVAL FOR CHILDREN
TOM BROWN'S FIELD GUIDE TO THE
FORGOTTEN WILDERNESS
TOM BROWN'S FIELD GUIDE TO CITY AND
SUBURBAN SURVIVAL
TOM BROWN'S FIELD GUIDE TO NATURE
OBSERVATION AND TRACKING
TOM BROWN'S GUIDE TO WILD EDIBLE
AND MEDICINAL PLANTS
TOM BROWN'S FIELD GUIDE TO WILDERNESS
SURVIVAL
TOM BROWN'S FIELD GUIDE TO LIVING WITH
THE EARTH

ABOUT THE AUTHOR

At the age of eight, Tom Brown, Jr., began to learn tracking and hunting from Stalking Wolf, a displaced Apache Indian. Today Brown is an experienced woodsman whose extraordinary skill has saved many lives, including his own. He manages and teaches one of the largest wilderness and survival schools in the U.S. and has instructed many law enforcement agencies and rescue teams.

TOM BROWN'S FIELD GUIDE TO THE FORGOTTEN WILDERNESS

Tom Brown, Jr.

Illustrated by Jackie McGuire

BERKLEY BOOKS, NEW YORK

TOM BROWN'S FIELD GUIDE TO
THE FORGOTTEN WILDERNESS

A Berkley Book / published by arrangement with
the author.

PRINTING HISTORY
Berkley trade paperback edition / April 1987

ISBN: 0-425-09715-3

BERKLEY®
Berkley Books are published by The Berkley Publishing Group,
a member of Penguin Putnam Inc.,
200 Madison Avenue, New York, New York 10016.
BERKLEY and the "B" design
are trademarks belonging to Berkley Publishing Corporation.

15   14   13   12   11

DEDICATED TO:

Kip Koehler, a true naturalist, philosopher and conservationist, who is trying desperately to save a small piece of wilderness at the edge of the world's largest megalopolis. To him I dedicate the Forgotten Wilderness.

Special thanks to Karl Kehde for his support and his fight to create a world where people and nature blend, to Frank and Karen Sherwood for their continuous unconditional friendship and love, to Frank (Wolf) and Lisa Rochelle for their relentless and tireless work, to Karlis (Bear) Povisils for his strength and spirit, and most of all to my wife, Judy, my sons, Paul and Tommy, and my daughter, Kelly, whose unconditional love and devotion through the darkest time in my life stood by me and made my dreams reality.

CONTENTS

x   *Contents*

GRANDFATHER, GREAT SPIRIT,
GRANT THAT I MAY FEEL THE RAPTURE
IN YOUR LITTLE THINGS
THAT I DO WHEN I GAZE UPON
YOUR GRAND VISTAS.

—Stalking Wolf, *May 1959*

TOM BROWN'S FIELD GUIDE TO THE FORGOTTEN WILDERNESS

INTRODUCTION

We had arrived the previous day at one of our favorite camping areas, one we usually visited only a few times a year. After building our debris huts and fires, locating our water source, and collecting some food, we sat around working crafts that would make our survival stay easier. The day was absolutely gorgeous: warm sun, gentle fragrant breezes, and the singsong chants of birds and insects—a flow of late summer life that made the senses swoon. It was a picture-perfect day, full of the wonders of nature and the potential for exciting explorations and adventures. The Pine Barrens were so alive and yet soothing; we could hardly ask for more.

Rick and I grew up in the Pine Barrens under the tutelage of Rick's grandfather, Stalking Wolf. Stalking Wolf was a displaced Apache, separated from his homelands by choice so that he could be with his family. Though he was at heart a wanderer, he chose to stay with us, to teach us, for we showed an incredible lust for knowledge of the wilderness and the "old ways." He'd originally planned to visit Rick for only a few weeks but ended up staying a little over ten years. Because Stalking Wolf wanted so desperately to pass on his knowledge before he passed away to the other side, we must have been the answer to a long-held prayer. I loved Stalking Wolf as if he were my real grandfather and I would indeed always call him Grandfather, not only to confirm the kinship between us but also to give the respect due to an elder and teacher.

Grandfather didn't want the old ways to die with him so he taught us, lovingly, with a method called *coyote teaching*. Coyote teaching is not done through rote or memorization but through trial and error, and experience. Its lessons are for all of the senses and seek to instill in the student an insatiable, inner need for knowledge. Each lesson holds tremendous spiritual ramification and aspires to many levels of understanding, some far beyond what is expressible in mere words. To Grandfather, nature was the university and the temple of the Creator, and each element of creation a profound teacher on both a physical and spiritual plane. Grandfather considered himself only a guide or catalyst to our learning, one whose task was to urge observation and the patience to grasp the profound, multifaceted and essential truths of nature.

One experience, in particular, exemplifies the aims of Grandfather's coyote teaching and how far-reaching that type of teaching can become. The lesson took place in the Pine Barrens only a year after we had begun to learn from Grandfather. Basically the lesson involved awareness. It was of critical importance to Grandfather that we should learn total awareness—of the landscape and all its creatures. Simply stated, you cannot be a good survivalist or tracker without a tremendous awareness of the natural world. Grandfather admonished us every time we passed anything—little flowers, nearby animals—without taking notice.

On this particular day, we were walking down one of the trails that connected my home to the main camp area where we spent most of our time. Because Grandfather taught by example instead of words, we never took our eyes off of him. We were always afraid that we would miss something profound. And so we would watch his head and if he would turn to look at something, we would do the same. Nothing he did escaped our notice; we did not want to appear foolish by passing by something obvious. We would walk behind him at some distance, not only out of respect and the fear that we wouldn't be able to watch him carefully enough if we were too close, but also because he said that we were too loud and scared off many things in our excitement.

As we passed under a rather large pine tree, Grandfather

turned around and said, "Don't disturb him." We were flabbergasted and embarrassed. What could we have possibly missed? We looked all around, especially at the ground, as that was where Grandfather was looking when he passed this spot. For the life of us we could not find anything—that was, until Rick looked up. To our stunned amazement, there, not ten feet over our heads, was a huge great horned owl. We had never been that close to an owl before, and we were utterly paralyzed by excitement until I realized that I had never seen Grandfather take his eyes off the ground. I was no longer interested in the owl but in how Grandfather could possibly have known without looking up that the owl was in the tree.

We ran to him, pleading with him to tell us how he knew that the owl was in the tree. At that point, a normal teacher would have taken us through the lesson by hand, pointing out every nuance until we had, at best—and if we remembered everything—a vague understanding of the owl. Grandfather, being a coyote teacher, answered simply, "Go ask the mice."

We did not see Grandfather for months after that. (He would frequently disappear while we were pursuing our lessons so that his presence would not influence the outcome or make it easier for us. Remember, that for the coyote teacher, the essence of a lesson lies in the experience of trial and error.) For months we lay on our bellies, watching the mice, learning everything we could, until I had bloody knees and a thick callus across my chest. Only then did Grandfather return to take us on to more advanced lessons.

What we learned from watching the "mice people" was simply incredible. No book or teacher in the world could have given us the kind of understanding we gained. We discovered what the mice would do when the owls were around, and what they would do when *any* predators, or nonpredators, were about. Moreover, we saw the reality of the food chain firsthand as the mice ate the vegetation and the predators ate the mice. But most important, we learned the profound lesson of the "concentric rings": *Nothing* can move in the natural world without affecting *everything* else. This was how the Apache scouts would learn the whereabouts of anything in the landscape. They would wait and watch for concentric rings thrown off by various entities moving about the landscape. With this method, it was not difficult to know the whereabouts, and direction, of a small band of men moving across the landscape fifteen miles away—or to understand how Grandfather knew the owl was in the tree without looking up.

Grandfather taught us also the great spiritual lesson of Oneness. He said that it wasn't enough to just be a part of nature, but we needed to be one with creation, at once a part and all parts, where there is no inner or outer dimension, nor separation of self from the natural world. This is what led me to say, in *The Tracker*, as we caught the rabbit in the snare, "The rabbit moved within the realm of Creation, and Creation moved within the realm of the rabbit." With everything Grandfather led us to, the meanings were always multileveled and profound. Meaning runs far deeper than the physical; things I thought I understood years ago have greater meaning today. Yet in all my years of wandering with Grandfather, the most majestic teachings came from the little things of nature, not the grandiose vistas.

As Rick and I sat and worked that second night in the Pine Barrens, we were engaged in conversations about the future. We each had visions of how we wanted to see and explore all this country's grand wonders, visions of the Grand Canyon, Yosemite, the Everglades, and the Black Hills. By comparison, the Pine Barrens seemed uninteresting and because we had spent so much time there, a bit boring. We felt that we knew the Pine Barrens quite well and that the prospect of new discovery was slight. Grandfather had been sitting nearby listening without comment to our conversation. We urged him to come over and tell us of the grand places he had lived and some of his adventures in the more awesome parts of the world. This was the beginning of one of the greatest lessons of my life, one I will never forget.

Grandfather told us that he had recently taken one of the most fascinating journeys of his life, one that rivaled anything we were talking about. We listened to his every word, imagining some wild and distant place as he described an exotic junglelike setting with huge herbaceous trees. In this jungle there were all manner of creatures, some docile, some very dangerous; boulders were of pure quartz; and the perils and adventures of this place were utterly fantastic. We listened for hours to the description of this place, yearning to go and visit it, for it was like no other place we had ever heard about before. When his story was finished, we asked him where this paradise was located. He said plainly, "Rick's front lawn."

We were floored. Never in my life had I ever heard anyone describe something as boring as a well-manicured lawn so enticingly. I scoffed at his words. "Go look at the lawn," was all he replied.

And so we would upon our return from the Pine Barrens, but all I could think of was how boring it would all be. I knew also that whenever Grandfather asked me to sit or look at something, it usually meant for quite a few hours. So I resigned myself to his instructions, and Rick and I went to his house. Grandfather placed us in the center of the lawn and told us to lie on our bellies. What unfolded before me was an adventure more intriguing, more vividly alive and wonderous even than what Grandfather had described.

Within moments I was hopelessly lost in this jungle of grass. I saw shapes, colors, textures, and things I could never have imagined. There was a whole world down there that I would not have believed could be so beautiful or intriguing. Tiny plants and fungi littered the grass forest floor. Miniature stones took on odd shapes, colors, and textures; some were dark brown, others black, some even crystal clear. The very earth itself was a marvelous blend of tiny jewel-like boulders, minuscule tracks, bits of plants, and sundry other mysterious items. The earth was littered with bits and pieces of the animal world: insect parts, hair, claws, whiskers, tiny teeth, bits of skulls. There were seeds of all descriptions, flower parts—so many other things that a list would easily fill a notebook.

More intriguing still was the life and death struggle going on right under my nose. Wolf and jumping spiders stalked the grasses for unsuspecting insects, bringing them down as a mountain lion brings down a deer. Denizens fed on plants, some burrowed into the earth and some laid eggs on the underside of plants. All this activity, beauty, intensity, and variation of life was found in barely a square foot of lawn. Never had I realized how much life I passed by every day without seeing. I understood fully from Grandfather's lesson that I could find a beauty and rapture of the senses anywhere I looked—if only I knew how. I will never again pass by even the most mundane landscape without knowing the myriad of things that are there, beyond man's conceitful eye.

I learned that I didn't have to go to distant, exotic places, to find the grand vistas. By training myself to see, to break down some old prejudices, I found the splendor of nature in the "forgotten" wildernesses. The problem with most people today is that they seek the ultimate thrills and the grandiose entertainment even when they venture outdoors. We mistakenly admire the person that has toured the greater wonders of the world and ignore the people who seek out the little pockets of nature. And yet those who know how to look close possess a greater understanding of the oneness of nature. When they do finally face the grand and beautiful panoramas, they will know them in a much deeper way. They will fully understand the connection between the grandest mountain and the smallest blade of grass, and how each is dependent upon and a reflection of the other.

WHY THIS BOOK

I sit at the edge of a pond watching, listening, as nature's splendor unfolds before me. The cries of redwing blackbirds blend with those of other birds to create a beautiful melody, this and the whispering of the winds, the chorus of frogs and insects, and the flutter of minute wings, all combine to make the symphony of the pond. Around me are flashes of color from flower and feather; thick, lush borders of green edge the pond and blend with the greenish waters. The surface of the pond is broken by thousands of tiny splashes created by insects, fish, frogs, and whirling swallows. Ducks drift across the surface, tipping up every once in a while to feed, and turtles sun themselves on half-submerged logs. This little pond setting could take place in any wilderness area but in this instance it is found just twenty yards from one of the busiest roadways in the country.

We have been conditioned to divide the world into two entirely separate entities, one being the "natural" world with all its grand scenic beauty and the other the inhabited, or sterile, world of the cities and suburbs. "And never the twain shall meet." People feel that they have to travel great distances into the national parks or reserves to experience nature and its beauties. Books depict the wild and wonderful areas of this country, and television and magazines probe the depths of distant panoramas and monuments of creation. But there is hardly any material disclosing the treasures of natural beauty and phenomena that occur right in our own back yards. Falsely we have been led to believe that the natural world exists only *outside* our communities and that we must venture into these wilderness areas to truly understand.

This book has been written to show that you don't need to go far outside the home to see the wonders of nature, that we can be sensitive to all things and find beauty all around us whether in a city, a suburb, or a wilderness area. The splash of color from wildflowers growing in an abandoned lot is just as beautiful as when found in some far-off wilderness. The lives of animals are just as interesting in our city parks as those in the forests and jungles. All natural areas are our teachers and great sources of inspiration, learning, and beauty. We do not have to wait for the long trips into the far places; we can discover and enjoy nature every day.

Despite the fact that I was brought up on the edge of a grand wilderness area and have spent most of my life wandering the grandest temples of creation, I find that I am drawn to nature no matter what and where it is. I am fascinated by the abundance of beautiful natural things found alongside a busy highway on the grassy strip we call a median. To me, nature is everywhere, and I find it tremendously exciting that it lives right alongside man without being detected. Simply stated, you don't need to wait until you have a week off from work and a pack on your back to enjoy the natural. All you have to do is look around you to discover the natural world growing and flourishing right outside the place you work, live, or play. It is there for everyone if you know how to look.

My hope is that this book will become a guide to the secret haunts of nature that are with us every day. My aim is to entice the reader into seeing the miraculous things that I see and to introduce the myriad signs, tracks, habits and habitats that are all around. I have spent hours watching the tiny creatures and beautiful landscapes found in a flower pot and the tracks that litter our yards and the median strips outside our offices. These clues open a new world that has been overlooked for all too long, a world that with the proper guidance can be appreciated once again.

PART I:
SUBURBAN WILDERNESS

Living in suburbia, one can easily feel alienated from the natural world. All around, houses give way to manicured lawns, sculptured hedgerows, and well-trimmed gardens. To the untrained eye, the area affords very little of the natural world, and nature-oriented residents find themselves lusting after trips into the country and wilderness areas. Time seems to stand still between these excursions abroad. With only a handful of weekend trips and infrequent vacations, people tend to resign themselves to the nature shows on TV or to the latest issues of *National Geographic*, *Sports Afield*, or *National Wildlife* to placate their longing.

What these suburb-bound naturalists fail to realize is that they are surrounded by an assortment of natural phenomena and beauty that rivals any national park or wilderness area. What lies beyond the confines of their walls is the secret world of nature just waiting to be discovered. In fact, so much happens in the suburban wilderness that it would take years to study thoroughly. The natural world has learned to blend with the suburban environments. It establishes strongholds in even the most highly trafficked places, and the animals have become suburbanites in their habits.

I find this world of suburban animals fascinating. Though their habits are basically the same as, or similar to, their wilder relatives, they have learned to adapt beautifully to a life near man, much the way man adapts to his particular surroundings and the ways of his community. Animals will develop skills and survival

11

standards specific to the environment in which they live. A raccoon that has lived its entire life in the suburbs would find it difficult to live in the wilderness and a wilderness raccoon would find it almost impossible to live in the suburbs. Each has its own set of codes and laws necessary for survival.

A good example of this adaptation ability is found in a study I have done concerning the deer along a stretch of the Garden State Parkway in New Jersey that runs through the Pine Barrens and terminates at Atlantic City. The parkway is a well-traveled, high-speed roadway that runs the length of the state. Anyone who drives that highway, especially at dawn and dusk, can't help but see tremendous numbers of deer feeding unperturbed along the sides of the road. Very few deer in this area are ever hit by cars, though their counterparts in other parts of the country seem to fair rather poorly. I set out to find the answer why.

First I studied the animals that were killed along that certain section of the parkway. On examination of their stomach contents and wear patterns of their hooves, I found that these animals were not native to that area. Many of them were males that had apparently wandered onto the road during the mating season. That spring and for many to follow, I observed the deer of the parkway, beginning with the young fawns and following their development to adulthood. These fawns I called the "parkway deer," not only because they were born along or near this roadway, but also because most of their lives were spent there. Most of their territory encompassed the edges of the parkway, and it was a most rich and varied feeding ground at all times of the year.

From birth, these animals are taught the lessons of the parkway. They are born to the din of rushing traffic and will most likely die to the same sound. They seem to sense when the busiest times will be and then, depending on the ebb and flow of the traffic, when it is safest to feed closer to the roadways. The traffic noise is to them much like the rush of a mountain stream to the wilderness deer, each familiar, each presenting its own specific dangers. The deer I studied were savvy in their knowledge of the road and how their lives were intertwined with it. Ironically, these parkway margins are really quite safe, for hunting is not permitted along any roadway of the state. Despite the noise, these deer were safe, happy, and well fed. Some of the grandest bucks I have seen in the Pine Barrens have been spotted near the parkway haunts.

Such deer have learned to adapt and survive, seemingly undisturbed, right next to a heavy traffic flow. Yet when other deer— those not born of the parkway—wander into the area, they usually end up as roadway carnage. Since my first study, I have watched generation after generation of parkway-born deer live and die. Only once did I see one die from being hit by a car and that was only when the driver lost control and crashed off the roadway. I realized that if these deer can live their lives and adapt to this heavily traveled roadway, then other animals can and will do the same. Everywhere man lives, animals have adapted their lives to fit in; those that cannot retreat farther into the wilderness or are eventually lost to extinction.

The deer living along the parkway were my first baptism into the changeable realms of animals. It became a truly fascinating subject that precipitated my looking more intently into the areas in which man would never expect to encounter many animals. What I found was a huge assortment of animals that live with us but have remained secretive because of survival purposes. One of my greatest thrills is to teach my students that the wealth of nature can be found everywhere. That even in these highly trafficked areas, the possibilities and thrills are endless, and the rewards as great, as in any wilderness area—without the travel.

Animals that live around the haunts of man tend to be more secretive and retiring than their wilderness counterparts, though there are exceptions. Raccoons found in suburban environments, for instance, will not run from man as readily as those in more untouched environments. This behavior depends, however, on the treatment those animals receive from their environment, including man. Raccoons that are shot or trapped for stealing garbage will, of course, be more retiring and skittish around man. The only simple, hard, and fast rule here is that man has no idea of the tremendous assortment of animals right outside his doorstep. This secret world of animals and plants will always remain hidden unless man learns to look deeper and appreciate more the little things of creation. A first step is to learn where and how to look; the second is to know what you are looking for and how it lives.

LAWNS

The first rays of the morning sun dance across the lawns causing them to glitter like some semitransparent, greenish glass. Droplets of dew sparkle and generate fiery rainbows. Small bejeweled spiderwebs look like tiny hammocks carelessly tossed across the blades. Because the tiny inhabitants are still chilled by last night's cold, there is no apparent movement in the grass. A robin alights momentarily on the shady lawn, then hops across to a sun splash. There, in the warm puddle of light, it pauses and cocks its head as if to listen or get a better view. Instinct tells it that the first insects or worms will begin to appear from this area as the sun stirs their inner fires and their cold blood warms to movement. Except for the robin, all seems frozen in time, dew, and sunshine.

The robin takes a few quick jumps forward, pauses for an instant, then pecks at the ground. There is a slight movement in the grass, and the robin pecks again, this time pulling a struggling worm from the earth. A few quick bounces and the robin is airborne, heading back to its nest, probably to feed its young. A good tracker knows that if a robin happens to eat the worm there on the ground, there are probably no young. Unless it suspects some predator is about, however, the robin will usually head straight back to the nest. By following the line of flight from a hidden position and repeatedly watching the robin collecting and feeding, the nest can easily be located and observed.

At this time I can either go back to the lawn for more study or get involved in the robin's activities. If I choose to stay with the robin for a while, I will make it a project that will last several days. For a long time, and at some distance, I watch the robin feeding her young. I do not want to alarm the mother, or interfere with the feeding schedule, but little by little, I move closer to the nest. This could take quite some time and a lot of patience, but it is well worth the effort. If the procedure moves into the second day, I will repeat the first day's efforts, only a little more quickly. With patience, and showing no threat to the robin, I will soon be accepted as part of the landscape, and the robin will go about its business as if I were not there.

I have had many intimate relationships with robins initiated in just this manner. On occasion, I have dug worms and fed the babies, apparently with the parent bird's approval. Sometimes the parent actually seemed relieved that someone else was helping with the task of feeding. One particular family of robins became my closest friends due to a good deed I once did while feeding the babies. When I first arrived one morning, I noticed a snake was making its way to the nest and the parent robins were frantically screaming. I quickly came to the rescue and removed the snake, releasing it far from the area. Early one morning, a few days after I had removed the snake, the mother robin began pecking frantically at my bedroom window. I ran from the house, following her to her nest, where I found another snake on its way up the lower branches. Again I intervened and removed the snake.

Over the next few weeks, the parent robin and I became close friends. It would wait patiently on my shoulder until I finished feeding the babies, then swoop down and lend a hand when I had finished. When I dug worms, it would be waiting right beside me, plucking out worms I would otherwise have missed. The summer quickly passed, but we remained friends through it all and I even helped the young learn to fly. It was like raising my own children, and I was proud of them all. Surprisingly, the next spring there came a tapping at my window, and there was my robin friend and her mate. They were in the process of building another nest, and I would watch for hours the whole process. Of course, I helped by gathering twigs and grass stalks, which they readily accepted, but they didn't like the way I weaved the sticks into the nest. Every time I placed in a stick, it was rearranged.

Despite my poor nest-building skills, the nest was finally completed, eggs laid, and I was a father again for another season.

Back at the lawn, the sun slowly dries the dew and the grasses warm and dull as the last of the lustrous dewy coat disappears. As the warmth begins to penetrate deeper, the inhabitants awake and begin to move. Lawns are like no other place on earth. They have an ambiance, a mood, and an appearance all their own. If, in fact, you could pretend that you were only an inch tall, the whole realm of the lawn would seem a beautiful but dangerous jungle. Long shoots of grass reach for the sun and form a canopy. Stems and blades intertwine into a thick mat to create darker and damper areas. Interspersed throughout all this greenery are the dead snags, those gray withered grasses that have fallen to the ravages of time, lawn mower, or insect and disease, and bits of tiny skeletons make a rich mattress of nutrients.

In the upper layer of seemingly endless grasses, there are other plants: crabgrass, broad-leafed plantain, dandelion, clover and myriad smaller plants and baby grasses. Some are so tiny, succulent, and soft that you can hardly feel them when you touch them. In the damper areas, tiny mushrooms and bits of moss or fungi grow. All this intermingling of rich greenery produces an almost impenetrable jungle, or forest, that would rival any in the larger world.

Throughout this jungle are series of trails and runs created and used by all manner of beasts. The floor is littered with all sorts of treasures. Some can be seen with the naked eye, while others can be seen only with a magnifying glass. Looking closely, tiny stones and pebbles take on gorgeous, faceted shapes. Some are transparent, others are crystalline, splashed with rich pastel colors that are rarely seen in the larger rocks of our world. Strewn about the ground are bits of insect wings, carapaces, antennas, and other parts. Teeth, claws, whiskers, hair, scat, and innumerable other objects litter the mats of dead vegetation and earth. All around, also, are the scrapes, dents, pocks, and scratches left by animals. Tiny and delicate tracks, etched so finely in the soils, are barely visible even with a hand lens.

Gazing into this intricately tangled moss of life, one can't help but realize the wealth of life found within every cubic inch. All over this miniature landscape is the evidence of animals, their feeding habits, life and death struggles, and numerous other signs that absolutely boggle the imagination. So many questions come to mind as the eyes eagerly consume every fragment. What made that mark? What caused this insect to lose its leg? What kind of egg casing is this, or what kind of seed is that? There are so many questions and it would take years to answer even the most obvious.

Sometime during the night, a white-footed mouse had passed over the lawn. It had not hesitated, for it was in a dangerous area, and though the lawn did contain things it would normally have eaten, the owls and other predators that hunted these areas would find the mouse an easy mark. I discovered the mouse's right rear footprint firmly planted between two small tufts of grass. Its feet had hit in such a way, due to its speed and the classic gallop pattern, that it landed in bare soil. The motion had shoveled the foot underneath the dead grasses that covered the bare earth, thus creating a tiny cave. It was in this tiny cave that I noticed a small wolf spider, apparently resting after a long night's hunt. Though the wolf spider is not a nest builder, it will take refuge in small holes and under various other litter. This little mouse-foot cave seemed to do the trick and kept the spider out of the sun. Last night had been cold, so I suspect that hunting had not been good. Most of the spider's prey would have been made a bit sluggish by the cold night air; wolf spiders prefer to hunt at night when their prey are active but will hunt during the day when the opportunity arises.

I carefully watched this little spider for over an hour. Every time a small ant passed by, the spider would position itself as if to strike. It seemed, however, that nothing that passed met its fancy. Finally, a large house fly landed on a fresh rabbit dropping that lay nearby. Cautiously the spider slipped from its cave and disappeared around a tuft of grass. Sticking to the shadows, it edged closer to the fly, which appeared to be absorbed in tasting. Within a few inches of the fly, the spider sprinted, pounced, and bit the fly on the abdomen. The fly slowly died, and the spider began to drag it back to its little cave. For the longest time, the spider tried to get the remains of the fly into the little cave but to no avail. They were both just too big to fit into the cave at the same time.

Watching the spider was another predator, a mud dauber.

Though the food for the adult wasp is nectar from plants, the food for its young are spiders, and this little spider was just what the wasp needed. The wasp had just completed another chamber of its nest, which was located under the eve of an old garden shed. Using the mud from a small puddle at the edge of the lawn and mixing it with its saliva, the wasp had carefully constructed each chamber of the nest. Into one of these chambers, it will pack spiders that have been anesthetized by its sting—the wasp's answer to refrigeration—lay its egg on the spiders, and seal off the chamber. As the young grow, they will feed on the spiders that are still alive and fresh.

The wasp landed on a dried plantain leaf not far from the spider's mouse-foot cave and from there it watched the spider struggling with the carcass of the fly. Slowly, cautiously, the wasp stalked toward the spider, her antennas feeling out in front as if to test the air for possible danger. With one powerful leaping flight, she pounced on the spider and attempted to turn it over. The spider responded to the attack with an evasive lunge, then countered by trying to bite the wasp on the abdomen. The battle lasted for the better part of a half hour, both opponents avoiding the sting or bite of the other, but each showing signs of weakening. The struggle crashed through the grasses and disrupted the miniature landscape, the sounds falling faintly on the ears of a shrew.

The shrew was hidden in a small rocky tunnel near a rock garden close to the battle area. The shrew's hearing is acute but its eyesight poor, so it cautiously began stalking in the direction of the noise. With short bursts of speed, it narrowed the distance between itself and the battle by darting through the grass tufts. Attempting to get a better look at the disturbance, it approached nearer to the battle, concealing itself behind the thicker grasses and the tunnel network that wove through the area. With one pounce, it entered the area of the struggle but missed its mark. The spider quickly retreated to the grasses, and the wasp took flight. In a futile attempt, the shrew jumped at the wasp as it became airborne but missed again. Caution, probably from the memory of other wasp and spider bites, kept the shrew from pursuing its quarry any farther, and it headed back to its little damp cave in the rock garden.

Nearing the mouth of its tiny enclosure, the shrew detected

another sound coming from a nearby grass pile. This little pile lay next to the corner of the rock garden and was a natural catchall left by the lawn mower every time the lawn was cut. It was a damp area where all manner of worms and insects took refuge from the hot sun. It was also one of the shrew's favorite hunting areas. Again, the shrew cautiously approached the origin of the sound. It was a little more careful than it had been during the wasp and spider battle. This time there was no fight to cover up the sound of its approach, and sensing this brought on a certain physical cautiousness: nose twitching, ears cocked, and eyes squinting.

It entered the darkness of the grass pile, following its nose and ears to the sound. In a small room that had been a nest for a common vole, it sensed a salamander feeding on an insect. Without hesitation, the shrew pounced on the back of the salamander, biting the neck hard. Even though its bite is slightly poisonous, it seemed to take a long time for the salamander to die. When at last it did, the shrew did not remove its prey from the little chamber but decided to devour it there. Voraciously, it tore at the flesh until there was hardly anything left except parts of the viscera, the head, the spinal column, and parts of the legs and feet. While the shrew rested near the tunnel digesting the meal, a carrion beetle began to feed on the salamander carcass. Because the shrew has to eat almost three times its weight every day, it went back to the carcass for one last bite but ate the carrion beetle instead. With a quick run, it exited the tunnel and headed back to its little cave where it would take a short snooze before hunting again.

Hovering just above the grass pile was a female sparrow hawk. It had seen the shrew enter the pile and the movement that signaled its return for the beetle. Patiently, it waited on vibrating wings, watching carefully every sign that would indicate when the shrew was on its way home. Instinctively the sparrow hawk knew that it had only a moment in which to catch the running shrew, for its den was not far away and it was very fast. Also, the surrounding grass and rocks afforded many escape routes, so the dive had to be orchestrated perfectly. Suddenly the shrew scurried toward the den. Now, the hawk folded its wings slightly and dropped to a spot just in front of the opening. Instinct and experience told it that the strike would put the shrew right beneath its talons.

With a powerful pounce, it slammed the ground, grasping the shrew firmly in its talons. There was no struggle from the shrew, for the hawk's sharp talons and bone-crushing pounce killed instantly. It stopped, looked around for a moment, then was quickly airborne, heading back to its nest located in a hollow tree at the far edge of the lawn, its young ones eagerly awaiting the food it brought. Because the hawk's young were not yet old enough to eat by themselves, it tore at the flesh of the shrew. It would be only a matter of days before they would have the skill—and be of a size—to swallow such a catch whole. After a short rest, the hawk flew off again in search of another meal to feed its young.

At the far end of the lawn where the hedgerow met the grass and the lawn mower couldn't reach, a strip of lawn grew a little taller, making a good home for innumerable insects and animals. It was from this grass area that the mouse I met earlier had run, leaving in its wake the deep print used by the wolf spider for a temporary shelter. In fact, this grass fringe was the home of many of the larger creatures that hunted or foraged the lawn. And it was in this hedgerow that the robin had made her nest. Most of the other resident birds also used this hedgerow as a resting, roosting, and nesting area. On the edge of the grass fringe, a garden spider had spun its web, for it was here that the most insect activity takes place. The spider hung upside down on the zigzag center of the web, vibrating back and forth rapidly into a blur so as to become invisible anytime a bird or other danger came too close to the web.

The day before, a weasel had killed a young chipmunk near the grass strip but abandoned it before its meal was finished. Flies buzzed about, laying their eggs on the carcass, and maggots had begun to appear. One fat fly inadvertently flew into the corner of the spider's web and struggled violently to free itself. Sensing the struggling vibrations, the spider ran to its prey, stunned it with a bite, then wrapped it in silken web. The spider dragged it to the center of the nest, where it drained the fly of its life juices. This argiope spider had taken over this location from another of its kind when the original spider had been eaten by a local boat-tailed grackle. The new spider had built its web overnight, defending its territory from other smaller argiopes to insure its survival. A good nest location means greater chances of survival because of newer food sources.

After eating some of its meal, the argiope began repairing breaks in the nest caused by the small cottontail that had wandered through it the previous dawn. The work went quickly but the argiope rested frequently so as not to draw attention to itself. Any spider knows that any unduly drawn-out motion will only attract attention, making it vulnerable to predators. Many times I have adopted the local argiopes as pets, feeding them partially stunned flies and other insects that I have collected. There is no need to take them from their web and place them in a cage. As long as the food supply holds out, they will stay in the same location. They will even get used to your presence.

At my farm, on the outer corner of the lawn, there are many argiope nests. I have named many of the spiders, and they stay around all summer. Two spiders in particular know that when I show up, they are going to get a free meal, and they will actually run to the corner of their web and await my handout. One spider in particular takes the offering right from my hand; it happens to be the largest in the patch because of the amount of food I give to it. I have even gotten to a point where I can carefully stroke its abdomen, and it seems to love it. After a meal, it will raise its back legs and wait for me to pet it, never moving until I am done. Sometimes if I don't pet it enough, it will crawl up on my hand and refuse to leave until I pet it some more.

The cottontail that broke the spider's web is a usual inhabitant of the lawns and lives in a brushy corner of the hedgerow. It has a nest of four young cupped in some of the longer grasses near the hedgerow. From here it leaves the thicker grass cover and ventures out onto the lawns in the evening to feed. Except the occasional neighborhood dog, the cottontail has few natural enemies in this suburban lawn. Most larger hawks, owls, foxes and other predators do not come this close to humans. The cottontail will, however, still use a great deal of caution when traveling or feeding, just as its wilderness counterparts do. It only came out in darkness to feed but could be seen at dawn and dusk by any careful observer. If I take the time to look closely to the lawn, I will see the tiny roundish scat that litters the ground. Or if I look at the ends of some of the more succulent clover and grass stalks, I may find the sharp forty-five-degree cut that indicates the cottontail or another rodent has been feeding.

Other animals come to the lawns from the longer edge grasses and overgrown patches. At all times of the day or night, you can find voles, mice, and chipmunks foraging the grasses for succulent shoots or seeds. Snakes glide across this green sea in search of insects or other creatures of the night, and assorted toads do the same. In summer and winter squirrels will forage the lawns for stray nuts and seeds, while all manner of birds comb the lawns for insects, seeds, or succulent shoots.

The lawn is not a dead or uninteresting expanse of green there to decorously frame our homes, but a sea of life more complicated and intricate than any of our larger realms. Many—animals, birds, insects—*depend* on the lawn for survival. It is constantly awash in the motion of life, a grand provider of food, always a source of wonder and beauty.

ANIMAL LIFE

Starling (*Sturnus vulgaris*)

The starling is an import from Europe and though found in many areas of the country, it can be seen in small flocks on our lawns during most times of the year. It is a very beautiful bird, appearing to be made of highly polished, iridescent dark metal. In the winter it sports an assortment of speckles but loses these in the summer and turns more blackbird-like. In the spring, the dark bill turns a bright yellow.

Scouring huge sections of our lawns, it forages voraciously for insects and seeds. Watching the feeding starlings, one realizes how they affect our smaller song birds. The starling leaves nothing unturned in its search for food and, in fact, is one of the single most powerful forces in the lawn's food chain. A small flock can work an average size lawn for several weeks, in the process greatly reducing the number of available insects and seeds. They seem to me to be much like a vacuum or lawn mower in their habits. Many people find them repulsive, not only because of

Starling

what they have done to our songbirds, but also because of their greedy attitudes.

Starlings will nest in birdhouses, tree cavities, or under the eves of houses and buildings. They prefer cavities and are evident by the droppings and debris left during the nesting season. Starlings can raise one to three broods per year, depending on the climate. Their eggs range from pale blue to whitish and glossy, with usually three to eight eggs in a nest, depending on food availability. Incubation is by both male and female and it usually takes up to fourteen days for a brood to hatch. It is in these nesting sites that you can get the closest to the starlings. They soon get used to your presence and become very tame for a wild bird. You will find that they will mimick other birdcalls, but not to the extent of the mockingbird.

I usually befriend the starlings at my farm during nest-building time by providing them with nesting materials. I collect grasses, straw, and small sticks, and place them on my bird feeder. After a few days, as the local starlings begin to take the nesting handouts, I begin to move closer and closer to the feeding table. I find that, within a few days, I can stand motionless by the table or lie on the lawn and they will come within inches of me. At the time when the eggs are about to be laid, some of the starlings will actually take the nesting material from my hand. One pair, nesting in the eves by my chimney, readily accepted my handouts right by their nesting hole, reaching out to me for more material as they built their nest. Remember though that it takes quite some time standing motionless to gain the confidence of the local starlings.

The starling can be a great deal of fun to study, but I like to keep in mind that they have been introduced late to this country and are in good part responsible for the diminishing songbird population. And so while I might stalk them and at times help in their nesting activities, I try not to do too much to encourage excessive propagation or make life too easy. Keeping this in mind, this is one of the easier birds to study and get to know, well worth the long wait and extra effort.

Robin (*Turdus migratorius*)

Who doesn't know the familiar robin, usually seen walking with its classic erect stance as it searches for earthworms and other insects. Its dark gray back contrasts dramatically with its thick reddish breast. (Females usually have duller breasts than males, especially during the nesting season.) The head and tail of the male is blackish, appearing at times to be polished stone. The female's tail and head is usually grayer. (Young robins have speckled breasts colored with a rusty wash.) There is also a beautiful white bib that descends from the yellowish bill. And sometimes there is a white hatch around the eye and on the belly's underparts.

The robin's diet consists mainly of earthworms, when they are available. However, it will eat grasshoppers, crickets, locusts, tent caterpillars, cutworms, ants, cicadas, among other insects. A few times, I have even witnessed robins eating small snakes up to nine inches long. During the winter their diet consists principally of berries.

The nests are made of mud, small sticks, and grasses, and can be found in trees and shrubs, building eves, and under bridges. The nests can contain two to five eggs so blue they seem to match the sky. Sometimes both sexes will incubate the eggs but most often it is the females; the incubation period is from twelve to fourteen days. In the warmer climates, there will be two to three broods annually. Robins range over much of North America and can be seen in our cities, towns and farmlands, usually on the lawns.

My memories of the robin go as far back as I can remember. It was the first bird name I ever learned and was the first animal I touched after Grandfather taught me to stalk. The robin has always had a special place in my heart. To most people, they are a definite sign of spring, but to me, they are so much more. Each time I see one, I remember all those young birds I have fed and all the adults I have touched.

Mockingbird (*Mimus polyglottos*)

The mockingbird is gray and about the same size as the robin, though sometimes a bit larger, and it is slimmer and has a longer tail. The large white wing and tail patches are very conspicuous in flight. The mockingbird can be found around our suburban homes utilizing the ornamental shrubs for roosts and the lawns for feeding. Mockingbirds seem to get along quite well with the small birds, such as chickadees or sparrows, rarely stopping to pick a fight, but it will defend its territory from other mockingbirds and drive off birds of similar or larger size.

Its nests are usually built around buildings and in trees and shrubs and located from three to ten feet above the ground. The outer nest is made of twigs; the inner part is lined with finer materials, such as grass and other fibers. Three to six eggs are laid in the nest. They are greenish to gray, sporting small red or yellow-brown spots. Incubation is primarily by the female, who is smaller than the male, and lasts about twelve days. Depending on the location, mockingbirds can have two to three broods a year.

In the spring and summer, their diet consists largely of insects—
flies, wasps, ants, bugs, spiders, caterpillars and grasshoppers,
among others—found in the lawns and shrubs around our houses.
In early autumn to winter, they change their diet to the fruits of
trees and shrubs, such as sumac, wild grape, honeysuckle,
Juneberry, virginia creeper, and mountain ash.

Mockingbirds are difficult to stalk because they are very aware
of their surroundings. However, mockingbirds will usually stake
out one territory for life, and if it is your home, you can coax
them onto the windowsills. With patience some will even take
food from your hands. A nesting mockingbird is a welcome addition to the ambiance of your yard; their songs are quite beautiful
and will add to the melodies of the other songbirds already in
residence.

An old farmer who lived near where Rick and I grew up was
the first to introduce us to the mockingbird. We would sit on his
porch, and he would call a pair of mockingbirds down to him and
give them tidbits of food. Rick and I wanted a mockingbird of our
own and spent the better part of the summer trying to entice our
local mockers every chance we got. I wish that I could say that it
only took a few weeks to get them eating from our hands, but it
actually took all that summer and well into the fall. Not until
winter was fast upon us did we finally gain the mockingbird's
confidence enough to have it come close and feed. Once we did
make contact, however, there seemed to be no getting rid of it.
Many times during the next summer it would become so brazen
that it would actually feed from our table during family picnics.
The number of people watching made no matter, though at least
Rick or I had to be present. I guess that we were a sign to him
that all was well and he was invited.

Garden Spider or Argiope (*Argiope aurantia*)

The argiope is not common to our lawns but is to the vegetation
and shrubs and fringe areas surrounding these areas. The rear of
the large body is black with bright orange or yellow spots forming
a band along the sides. The front legs are usually as long as the
entire body. Nights are usually spent rebuilding the web, a
structure up to ten feet across with a zigzag pattern near the

center, where the adult hangs upside down. When disturbed, the spiders will drop from their web and run into the underbrush to hide. Many times you can watch the spiders bounce back and forth on their webs much like a sideways trampoline. These remarkably strong webs, with only certain sticky parts, are usually built in sheltered areas away from the wind. The male and female build similar nests, and both are capable of killing insects as large as grasshoppers. Eggs are laid in the early fall in a paper cocoon, about the size of a hickory nut, which is fastened to the surrounding vegetation.

There was once an argiope at the corner of our garden facing the lawn. I was fascinated by this spider because it was so large in comparison to the other spiders I had seen during my travels. It soon became a pet, and I would feed it whenever I caught an insect I thought it might like. There was no need to put the spider in a container, because between my feedings and the

Garden Spider

naturally good hunting at its web site, there was no need to move on. It grew to know me quite well and would not hesitate to climb on my hand to take a fly from my fingers. It even liked to be petted, but because it could bite, I was always cautious.

This spider was always a source of wonder. I used to lie by it for hours as it built the nest, utterly fascinated by its abilities. There was such beauty in both its movement and its gorgeous coloring. It seemed such an intricate blend of black and yellow, producing an exotic combination of markings. We grew to trust each other so much that I could easily approach the nest without disturbing it, while other people would cause it to run. One day, however, it was eaten by my tame mockingbird, apparently out of jealousy. The mocker never liked the time I spent at the web. During that summer, two other spiders attempted to build their nests in the same location, but the mocker would not allow it. The mocker would touch no other web in the area, only the spiders attempting to build on the original site.

Wolf spider (*Family lycosidae*)

One or more species of the wolf spider probably live in your area. Though they tend to prefer areas of thicker growth, they can be found hunting on your lawn. They are medium-size spiders, usually gray in color, but can be yellow, grayish-brown, or brown with a yellow middle stripe down their backs, and have rather short, stout legs. They usually run on the ground without making nests of any sort, though the female builds a silk-lined nest for shelter in the early summer. They are commonly found resting under stones or in small holes in the ground, but can move quite rapidly if the need arises, even across water and, at times, will even dive under water to escape a pursuer.

The food of this spider is primarily insects caught on the run. Though the wolf spider can be active during the day, it usually prefers to hunt the grasslands at night, when its game is more active. Wasps are one of its primary enemies, since the wasp uses the wolf spider as food for its young. A fight between a wasp and a wolf spider can truly be something to watch—fierce and some-times lasting up to an hour.

At home, in my terrarium, I used to keep a few wolf spiders as pets, and they seemed to thrive. I would bait the terrarium with honey or a small piece of carrion to draw flies from the house into the terrarium so that the spiders always had a ready supply of food. When camping, Rick and I would keep them for study in a large jar in our camp areas. We were surprised once when a female we had caught was carrying an egg sac (near the rear of its body). From just that one wolf spider, we ended up with thirty-five full-grown spiders by summer's end. They are tremendous spiders to watch and enjoy, especially their hunting and stalking techniques.

Grass spider (*Agelenopsis naevia*)

The grass spider is probably one of the most common spiders of our lawn. It is medium-size and varies in color, but it has two long black lines bordered with gray that run lengthwise along the back. The legs do not vary greatly in length. They live only one year, the winter being spent in an egg stage, the adults dying soon after eggs are laid.

They are usually found on or near their webs, which are built on the grass. Many grass spiders will stay on one web all summer if not disturbed—webs of the grass spider are used by some birds in nest making—with the web enlarging as the season progresses. Unlike most spiders, the grass spider will run to the top of the web when threatened, and hide in a funnel. This funnel has a rear escape from which the spider can pounce upon its prey. The webs of the young spiders can be seen as early as May and are particularly visible when covered with dew or dust.

Although sometimes preyed upon and caught by parasitic wasps, the grass spider's sensitivity to their environment is incredible, enabling them to sense the presence of even the smallest of insects on or near their web. Once Rick and I counted (and named) seven individuals that remained on their webs throughout most of a summer. Unfortunately, these spiders were not as tame as our wolf spiders and garden spiders.

If your terrarium is large enough, they do make excellent pets. Since these spiders tend not to become tame, this may be the best way to study them at close hand.

Earthworm

Earthworm (*Lumbricus terrestris*)

The earthworm is one of the most common inhabitants of our lawn—encountered while gardening, fishing, digging or after a hard rain—but it is amazing how little people know about them. They can grow up to eleven inches long and have a pointed head end and flattened tail end. Surprisingly, it is easy to tell the sex of an earthworm; those of the male are open at the fifteenth segment, while those of the female are open at the fourteenth. Tiny bristles underneath, coupled with secreted mucus, enable the animal to climb even the smoothest surfaces and to retract quickly into the burrow, its underground habitat, to escape danger. It favors damp soil and will burrow deeper underground when the lawns dry out. The earthworm usually feeds outside the burrow—mostly at night—on decaying organic matter. In some instances, however, where the ground is exceptionally rich in decaying vegetable matter, the earthworm will not have to leave its burrow at all and will actually feed through the ground.

During a heavy rainstorm, their burrows may fill with water, which forces the earthworms out. During light rains, they will suck in the soil and spew it out the top of their burrows, making a tiny pile of sculptured mud. If you look closely at the ground, especially after a rain, these little piles can be plainly seen.

Field cricket (*Gryllus assimilis*)

Crickets sing at night in most parts of this country. The smaller brown cricket, or field cricket identified by its three distinctive dark abdomen stripes, is probably the most common and can be found in fields, gardens, lawns and even houses.

The cricket will eat both plant and animal matter but prefers plants, usually grains and vegetables. Small holes in tomatoes, cucumbers, strawberries, and sometimes peas are good evidence of a cricket's presence in your garden. A cricket will also destroy clothing if given the chance. Crickets will spend their days lying in the moist areas under rocks or thick vegetation, at the lawn's edge, usually venturing out onto the lawn only during the evening hours when they are protected from most predators.

Crickets

The female cricket has a long, slender ovipositor (for the depositing of eggs) and will, in the late summer and fall, lay hundreds of eggs in holes in the ground. The characteristic cricket song is produced by the male rubbing its wings together, its purpose mainly to defy other males. Crickets chirp the loudest when the weather is clear and warm.

Grandfather used the nighttime cricket voices to teach Rick and I to locate the precise origin of a sound. We would listen for a cricket, stalk to where we thought the sound was coming from and, with the aid of a flashlight, try to locate the cricket. This helped us develop a hearing acuity that enabled us to pinpoint sound with dead accuracy. I kept crickets in my terrarium so that I could hear them sing at night. It was a way of bringing the outdoors inside. Because a cricket can be quite an indoor pest, great care must be taken to prevent it from escaping, if you decide to keep it as a pet. Also, I had to move my crickets from their original indoor location because they kept my parents awake.

Bumblebee (*Bombus spp.*)

Who has not encountered the black and golden-yellow bumblebee buzzing around our lawns? Bumblebees love fields of clover or showy, fragrant flowers. They also abound in orchards when the fruit trees are in bloom. The abdomen is usually very fat, with wings absurdly small—or so it seems. Their flight seems to be drowsy and a bit erratic. The female of the species is most abundant in spring or late fall, and the workers are found throughout the summer.

The queen lives through the winter and starts her new colony in the spring. She can lay from 400 to over 1,000 sausage-shaped eggs that will hatch into larvae in five days. The larva is hairless, wingless, and maggot-shaped, or vermiform, and is enclosed in a wax shell. In about six days, the larva is transformed into the pupa, an intermediate quiescent stage during which the larval structures of the insect are replaced by those typical of the adult bee. The pupa is encased in a strong cocoon and will hatch in about ten days. The larvae are fed honey and pollen. In late summer, the adult bees—males and new queens—develop and mate in flight. In the fall, a colony of up to 250 individuals may

Bumblebee

die except for the fertile queens, who will seek out a sheltered area for hibernation.

The nest of the bumblebee is usually a hole dug into the ground, constructed in good part of moss and a tremendous amount of grass. It is not uncommon to see an adult bumblebee cutting grasses from our lawns and carrying them back to the nest. The bumblebee and its nest are a favorite food of the skunk.

Rick and I first encountered a good specimen of a bumblebee for study when we found a queen wedged in the crevasse of an old tree one winter. We thought it was dead, but Grandfather explained that it was very much alive and well, despite its death-like appearance and the sub-freezing temperature. In hibernation, Grandfather explained, the queen is virtually immobile, appearing as if she were frozen to death. Because of this, winter is an excellent time for study. But, *Do not*, however, warm her body, and make sure she is put back *exactly* in the place you found her. If the bee is warmed and begins to move, there is still a possibility of getting stung. The bumblebee has a very powerful sting to which many individuals have severe allergic reactions.

Hospitalization may be necessary and in some cases death may result. I offer this simply as a warning to students to exercise caution when tracking the bee.

We always had a deep fear of the bumblebee, moreso than of any of the other stinging insects. Even though we had not, at that point, ever been stung, or even attacked, their huge size, heavy buzzing, erratic flight, and what we considered threatening gestures, frightened us. Despite this fear, we wanted to know more about this bee because he was always around and a source of intrigue, not only from its ominous appearance but also from its mysterious habits. Grandfather always encouraged us to get to know all types of animals; what we did not know, we would fear, and what we feared, we would ultimately destroy. That, he said, was the reason people killed snakes, coyotes, wolves, and various birds of prey. Their fear came from ignorance and, instead of improving the balance of nature, as they presumed, they were destroying the equilibrium of the whole realm. Fear, he said, was one of the reasons that the world was destroying itself.

Our fear of this bee was very real and our initial few encounters with it harrowing. At first we studied it at a distance, as it foraged nectar from honey. We always carried a bottle of water so that we could thwart any attack by dousing it. For months our observations were always at this safe distance, keeping close watch for any move that could be considered aggressive. Many times we would go running headlong through the most tenacious vegetation because we thought that we were being attacked. After a few months, Grandfather sat us down and asked us about the bumblebees. Unfortunately, we could hardly even answer the simplest questions, which indicated to Grandfather that we had not studied because of our fear.

Without saying a word about our fear or showing the least bit of disgust over our poor observation skills, he hiked us to a meadowsweet bush that usually swarmed with all manner of insects, especially the bumblebees. We sat down by the bush, visibly shaken by the close proximity of the swarming bees, which Grandfather immediately detected. Teaching us a lesson of stalking and the quietening of inner spirit, he matter-of-factly walked up to within inches of the flowery bush. The bees seemed to pay no attention. Slowly, in a flowing motion, he reached his hand toward the flower; the bees still cared little of his presence. He then plucked a flower cluster from one of the lower branches and held it still, close to his face. Within a few moments a bee alighted on the flower and began to forage the nectar. To the bee, Grandfather must have been nothing more than another bush.

We were shocked to see Grandfather's next move. Slowly, ever so carefully, he began to edge his index finger toward the feeding bee. The whole procedure seemed to take hours, and we found ourselves caught between excitement and holding our breath, sure that he would be stung at any moment. The bee got used to Grandfather's finger, and soon he was stroking the bee between the wings. The bee would stop foraging momentarily, as if to savor the touch. Within a half hour there were a half dozen bees that Grandfather had befriended and stroked, and not one showed any signs of aggression or attacking. On two occasions during the episode, he stroked a honeybee and a yellow jacket, with the same marvelous results.

A few days later, Rick and I got up the courage to try the same thing that Grandfather had done. We approached the bush the same way, held a flower, drew the bees, approached the bees in a stalking manner, but as soon as I touched the bee, I was stung unmercifully on the tip of the finger; moments later, Rick was stung twice. We were so upset that we had to find Grandfather and tell him of our plight and how miserably we had failed. He listened intently to our story. Every gory detail was described, and our miserable failure was written all over our faces and in our throbbing fingers. Grandfather applied a poultice made from some plantain, and the swelling and pain went down. As we relaxed, he told us what we had done wrong.

We had done everything the way Grandfather had, even going to the same bush, sitting in the same place, and holding the flower in the same way. We had even attempted to touch the bees exactly at the same speed and flow that Grandfather had used. Grandfather asked us what we were feeling when we had attempted to touch the bees. Were we still afraid, apprehensive, nervous, deep in thought, or were we full of love, friendship, and role-playing the plant which we held? Were we all of the former and none of the latter? The lesson hit home as assuringly as the shock of the sting. So many times Grandfather had told us to approach an animal as if we were empty, full of love, and showing them no harm and having no fear. We had broken all the rules and had learned a valuable lesson the hard way, as usual.

A few weeks after the initial shock of our failure had warn off, we tried to touch the bees again. It wasn't an overnight decision but a slow process of approaching the bush, getting close, sitting for long periods of time, and really getting to know the bees. Once our fear was abated and we could approach the bush with love and emptiness, we again held a flower cluster. This time I touched a bee, and he seemed to love it. I gently rubbed that portion between his wings, and he sat for a long moment relaxing, wings vibrating, as if languishing in the attention. I found that what we fear, we will never know, and what we don't know, we will eventually destroy.

Little black ant (*Monomorium minimum*)

One of the first insects you will probably encounter when you lie down on the lawn is the little black ant. This is one of the most common ants and can be found on lawns throughout the United States, and in the house and sandy places. These little ants work in definite paths throughout the lawns. Long lines of them can be seen going to and from work along established common highways. With the aid of a magnifying glass, you can see these highways quite clearly in the lawns and, upon closer inspection—and with a bit of patience—even the tiny footprints can be seen.

Ants are tremendous creatures to watch. Ants of any type, but especially the black ants, have always been a source of intrigue to me. They are so mystical in their movements and communication. I could literally lie on my belly for hours watching the goings and comings of ants. They seem to pause momentarily and touch antennas, which communicates the jobs that must be done. At first, their movements will seem aimless, but upon further investigation, you can establish a definite pattern of where they are going or what they are doing. My favorite, out of all the ants, are the ones I call the scout ants. Much like me, they'll seem to wander without regard for time or destination. It would seem they're in the greatest danger, but I like to think they have the most adventure.

Rick and I were always fascinated by the ants, not only because of their intricate travels, great strength, and incredible engineering feats, but also because we were also intrigued by how they could live so comfortably in a world prowled by the most vicious lawn predators. Their survival is due, in good part, to their superb sense of communication, and we could not help but marvel at the way the entire colony would work as if governed by some marvelous superconsciousness.

The little black ant taught us one of our most perplexing and necessary lessons in tracking, a lesson that made it possible to find and follow the most difficult tracks of other, often larger animals. The lesson, as always, came from Grandfather, who, whenever he approached a subject, always chose for us the most difficult route to learning so that, when we met the normal problems, we would excel. It was an old Apache saying that if you wanted to be a good man tracker, then track mice, but if you wanted to track anything else, then practice tracking ants. And so we did.

Black Ants

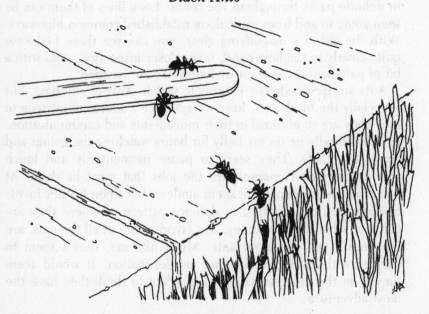

The wisdom of ant tracking came after a few years of attempting to track the general larger mammals. We were having great difficulty finding tracks in the heavy brush and on the hard-packed roadways; tracking on driveways and the edge of highways was impossible. When we finally asked Grandfather to teach us to pick out the tracks, he simply said, "Go track the ants."

At first, we were pretty skeptical of this advice, for we could not see *any* visible trail, even in the best of dusty conditions. We would lie for hours every day, on lawns, roadsides, dust patches, and beaches, but still the tracks of the ants would not reveal themselves. Even seeing an ant walking along a dusty path would not give us a clue as to where it left its trail. And so, after several weeks of this frustration we finally went back to Grandfather, a little embarrassed about our dilemma.

Grandfather solved our problem quickly, using some rather "modern" methods. He told us that we could not see the ant tracks because we had no idea of what to look for or what the tracks looked like. He told us to collect some chalk dust from school to use as a tracking medium; when he was a child, he ground up seashells to a fine powder for the same purposes. The next day we spread the chalk dust down on a piece of black construction paper, then painstakingly coaxed a few ants to walk across. There on the paper, like a beautiful and intricate tapestry, lay the ant trails, far different than what we ever expected. Our lessons were well taken and from then on we could easily see the ant trails in the dust areas of our haunts.

But we had to learn more from the ants. Sure, it was easy to track ants in the dust, but how about across the pebbles and tiny stones that made up most of the ants' roadways. Easily solved once again—Grandfather created a larger object lesson using us as the trackees. We walked along a gravel bed for quite some distance and then came back to "track" ourselves. At first it seemed impossible, but Grandfather pointed out the stones we had disrupted—the way the stones were ground together, were abraded, pushed in, flipped out, kicked from and skidded in their beds—we could finally track ourselves.

We then went back to the ants and found, after careful examination, that they had done the same things to the little stones that we had done to the larger stones. We could finally tracks ants—

with ease! With this lesson learned, we returned to the larger animals that had before proved so difficult to track and found we could now do so with deadly speed and with very few mistakes, even when the tracks crossed boulders and hard-packed driveways. Today, anytime I want to push my tracking skills, I go back to tracking the ants over the most difficult terrain I can find. This way, when I get to the larger animals, it becomes as simple as tracking an elephant across a beach. The ant people are truly special to me, not only because of their mysterious lives but also because they are the greatest tracking teachers of all time.

The winged females and winged males usually mate in the spring or fall. As with all ants, the queens lose their wings and then establish a colony in a burrow underground. The eggs of these ants can develop into workers, queens, or males. Workers will care for the queen and the larvae, and they will move the larvae and pupae around in the colony to places where the humidity and temperature are more suitable for their incubation.

HEDGEROWS

Bordering the lawns and gardens of our houses are the hedgerows. These rows of ornamental plants and various brush tangles house an incredible assortment of animals that use the lawns and other areas of our yards as foraging grounds. These hedgerows provide the cover and nesting sites of many of our local animals. Without these rows, the number of animals haunting our lawns would be limited to those that could find sufficient food and cover in the lawn alone. Generally, the more hedgerow and surrounding vegetation a lawn has, the more wildlife will be seen on the lawn itself. Whenever possible, we should maintain our hedgerows, thus increasing the habitat for animals that will visit our yards.

Inside the hedgerow is an exciting, mysterious world. Upon entry into any hedgerow, one experiences an astounding change in the light level, atmosphere, and sound. It feels as if we have crossed into a totally different environment, utterly removed from that of our yards. It feels as if we could be in any wilderness area of this country, far removed from what exists just outside the leaf cover. The light is diffused, splashing across the ground in an exotic mosaic of color and shadow. The plant growth is lush, and only those that like the low light levels and dampness survive. The temperature drops and humidity rises as soon as you enter these little cathedrals. The scent of dirt is rich and potent.

The sounds inside the hedgerows are intense. Most outside noise is diminished to a whisper; the sounds of birds, carried by the soft winds that seep through the leafy covers, drift around and through the brush. The hedgerows seem to be inhabited by layer. The upper vegetation is littered with bird nests of all shapes, sizes, and positions. The mid layer attracts smaller birds, chipmunks, and beautiful spiders and insects. The floor of this temple is inhabited by all manner of beasts. At times I feel as if I am lying in some exotic, sometime fearsome, miniature jungle, full of exotic birds, beasts, and plants.

The earth is usually covered by a rich, loamy carpet of leaves and debris. Moving through this carpet are some of the most wondrous insects and animals we can find in our yards. As you dig gently down, through the upper leaf cover to the more humid, dense undersoil, more and more animals and tiny plants are revealed. The realm of the carpet literally swims with life and has a magic all of its own. The possibilities for study are at once awesome and endless.

I can lie on my back, cradled in this world of the hedgerow, removed from the outside world as if in peaceful retreat. I'll stare up through the translucent, leafy ceiling, watching the dappling of dancing light and listening to the songs of the soft wind and rustling leaves. I seem to sink into the carpet and disappear from sight and can watch in peace the comings and goings of the upper dwellers. Here in the hedgerow I can get closer to the animals than in any other part of my yard, and here, also, I can be soothed by the Earth Mother's softness.

I watch the comings and goings of various birds as they build their nests, oblivious to my presence, unaffected by my interest. Some of the birds dance among the branches and sing to each other, entering and leaving this shelter through ever-shifting doorways and windows to the outside world. Other birds flit about the lower branches or forage through the leaf cover in their search for food. Warblers, sparrows, titmice, cardinals, robins, catbirds, and finches—the hedgerow is alive not only with their music, but also with the shuffle and rustling of their feet as they kick up the ground in search of tidbits.

I watch the antics of a catbird as it dances through the tangle, screaming its rasping c-a-t, c-a-t, call. At first, I think it is warning the surrounding bird world that a cat is near, but it is only scolding a garter snake that is making its way up through the lower branches. The snake had just finished swallowing a dead baby bird that had fallen from a nest and lodged in the lower branches. The garter snake usually eats cold-blooded creatures, such as frogs, toads, salamanders, and insects, but it is an opportunist and will sometimes eat baby mice or dead birds. The snake's skin appears bright and shiny in the broken sunlight, as if it were coated with glass. Sometime during the past few days, it must have shed its skin because it is shinier than normal, appearing almost wet. The birds don't think it is as interesting or beautiful as I do and have gathered in a small scolding flock. Some mockingbirds, dodging and weaving, peck at it and the snake soon retreats into the innermost recesses of the root tangles for peace.

The snake's entry into the small protected lower brush frightens a chipmunk that had been foraging for seeds and nuts. The chipmunk runs up the lower branches to escape but is greeted by the frenzy of birds, already excited by the snake. The chipmunk also beats a hasty retreat down its tunnel, which is beneath a forsythia bush. The chipmunk is a frequent occupant of the hedgerows, building its network of tunnels to live and to escape danger. There it forages for the nuts, berries, insects, and green plants that abound in the area. Once in a while, it will steal a baby bird from a nest for food—that is why it incurred the wrath of all the local birds. This particular chipmunk knew the area well and was wary of all the dangers of the area. The birds held no particular threat, but the local cats, and especially a weasel that lived a few hedgerows over, were its biggest fears. Otherwise, it lived a relatively carefree life among the shrubs and brush and, in fact, life was so good that it was a bit overweight compared to its wilderness counterparts. He wasn't at all above raiding the local garbage cans or bird feeders whenever the opportunity arose. He was also very tame and would take food from my hand.

Inhabiting the mid to upper branches of the hedgerows are a wide variety of insects including cicadas, katydids, walking sticks, mantis, beetles, and bark borers. Many of the local birds feed on this huge insect population. Throughout this upper portion of the hedgerow are miniature highways of ants and other insects, branches that serve as roadways and bridges. The insects know this network of roadways well and can live out their lives hardly ever touching the ground. From the web of animals that occupy the hedgerow's upper canopy to the verdant ground covering all niches are filled; all is rife with life's activity.

A daddy longlegs walks on his long spindly legs across the leaf litter in search of small insects or decaying plant matter for food. This spider is a confirmed wanderer, and makes no web. He blends beautifully with the colors of his surroundings and will appear suddenly, as if from nowhere. His carriage is graceful, walking seemingly on tiptoes over even the roughest terrains. I watch him, for a long time, weave through the leaf litter, probing here and there as he goes along. Once in a while he stops and bends forward toward the ground. His world is much too tiny for me to determine, at such a distance, his object but I would venture to guess that he was sifting out some edible tidbit. Such a sight always stirs my imagination.

Scratched into the leaves, like tiny pinpricks, is evidence of the travels of mice and other rodents. Some of the damper leaves show the still glistening mucus trails of snails. All about lies the fallen debris of the upper world—insect parts, egg casings, seeds of every description, rotted berries and leaves, animal hairs, teeth and bones. I dig down a bit and find a few sow bugs, some ants, and a millipede. Digging deeper, a centipede shoots across the hole and disappears quickly into the leaf wall at the other side. Deeper still I encounter a few worms, which retract quickly into their holes as soon as I lift the "roof." Spiders of all sizes and color patterns hunt these ground areas much like coyotes or wolves hunt in our larger world.

The fragrances that waft through these temples are, to me, both awesome and sublime, a thick, rich scent of damp loam mixed with the delicate bouquet of wild and cultivated flowers, cut lawns, and the scents of ornamental cedars. It's a smell I find intoxicating, exhilarating.

Flying insects permeate this jungle, vibrating the air at all levels. The whole dome of the hedgerow pulsates with life of every kind, on every level. The eyes cannot pick out an uninhabited place nor can the ears detect a pause in the overall music. Here is rest for the spirit, where the body can feel totally surrounded by life.

ANIMAL LIFE

Daddy longlegs (*Leiobunum vittatum*)

The daddy longlegs is an oft encountered inhabitant of our deeper hedgerows. It is not a *true* spider, though commonly thought to be. Its body is a beautiful deep brown, and its legs are black. The legs will vary in length from one to two inches with the second pair of legs, on the body, the longest. The male tends to be smaller bodied, but deeper in color than the female. The abdomen is segmented, unlike most spiders, and has a very effective stink gland, which is one of its main sources of protection. Daddy longlegs can also be found in fields and meadows, usually close to the ground, and have been known to congregate in considerable numbers in brush piles and in hollows, though they are primarily solitary.

The eggs are laid in the fall from a long ovipositor, which plants

Daddy Longlegs

the eggs deep into debris or underground. Most adults die before winter, after the eggs have been laid. The young hatch in the spring. They are white with black eyes but appear very much like the adults. The white soon changes to the adult colors.

The food of the daddy longlegs is tiny insects, animals, or other decaying matter. Generally, they love the nighttime, but may be active during the day. They move relatively slowly, and if grabbed by a leg, they will quickly shed it. They are virtually harmless to humans, but I've found they do not make good pets.

The best way to study the daddy longlegs is to approach one slowly in a stalking manner (see *Stalking*, Part IV). If you approach too quickly, the spider will only assume that he is being pursued and will run away. If you are persistent, however, and move slowly, the spider will eventually settle into his daily business and go about feeding or otherwise exploring its territory. You must look closely when they are feeding, for much of their food is very small; approaching them, ever so slowly, with a hand lens tends to be a big help in watching them feed.

After months of tracking the ants to hone our tracking abilities, Grandfather graduated Rick and me to bigger things, one of which was the daddy longlegs. The reason Grandfather chose the daddy longlegs was not so much the tracks themselves, which were easier to see than those of the ants, but because of their erratic, seemingly mindless way of walking. The daddy longlegs would follow no set pattern, nor would it allow leaves, twigs, bark, or even trees to disrupt its course. To find just one complete track, evidence of all eight legs in a set pattern, could take hours and following it for just a few inches could take a full day or more.

Nevertheless, the daddy longlegs was our next teacher. A teacher that would make us observe every shred of evidence and assume nothing unless the tracks proved it. The daddy longlegs taught us to think, to test patterns and to role-play—if I were a daddy longlegs where would I go? Why, how, and how fast? Nothing could be left to chance, for one missed step could mean losing the animal entirely. The daddy longlegs was a source of great frustration, but we eventually grew very fond of it. Like the ant, its teachings allowed us to follow the larger animal patterns no matter how intricate or complicated they became.

To us, the lawns and weed patches were sources of wonder, worlds apart from what we were used to in our everyday world. There we could get lost in a land of make-believe where all things became bigger than life, very scary, fascinating, and full of adventure. In our little world, the daddy longlegs was always the good guy, the troop transport, for he could cross terrain that would take the smaller animals hours to traverse. Just to see a daddy longlegs up close is a source of inspiration and utter amazement. Even today, I look at this spider as one of the most fascinating of the spider world. In essence, it must be an engineering triumph for I often wonder how it moves those wobbly legs so effortlessly over such tough terrain.

I will always be grateful to the daddy longlegs, not only for the pleasure derived from simply watching this creature, but also because of the proficient tracker it has made me today. Without the little black ant and the daddy longlegs, I doubt I would be able to read the microscopic pressure releases found in the larger tracks. To all beginning trackers, the best place to learn is not in wilderness, but in your own backyard, by following black ants and daddy longlegs. What they can teach you about tracking will surpass the lessons of even the greatest trackers that have ever lived. Truly, they are two of the most magnificent and fascinating teachers the Great Spirit ever created.

Millipede (*Julus spp.*)

Millipedes are common to the dark, moist environment of the hedgerow floor, but they can be found also in meadows or gardens in piles of decaying vegetation. Their eggs are laid in a small cluster in the damp earth. The young hatch in about three weeks and have only three pairs of legs, but as they go through successive molts, the number of legs and body segments increase to thirty or more parts. Their food is primarily decaying plant matter, but in wet weather, they may feed on the roots of many species of living plants. Millipedes protect themselves by curling into a tight coil so that the hard plates of their backs cover the soft underpart. Stink glands, located along the sides of the body, make the millipede unpalatable to most animals.

Rick and I were always fascinated by the millipedes (and also

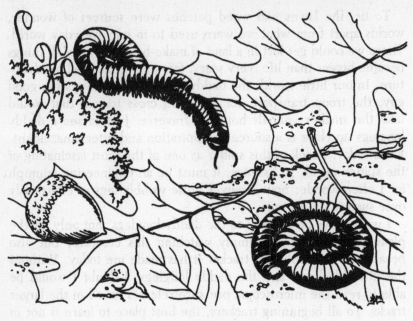

Millepede

the centipedes, which are not related but can be found in the same environment). The way these animals would weave their trails through the loam and leaf litter was always intriguing. They made their little trails and roadways slip down intricate tunnel networks and caves that were found in the leaf litter. Their movements were always so impressive, especially the coordination of leg activity when maneuvering in difficult terrain. Their movement at any time was graceful, undulating and very sure-footed. To us they seemed secretive, mythical little beasts from another world.

We regarded the millipede with the utmost respect, because Grandfather considered it a great teacher of the love of the earth. Of course the millipede posed a major tracking problem, but its trail was more definite than that of the little black ant and easier to follow than the daddy longlegs'. The tracking problem posed by the millipede was that it loved to crawl through the most tenacious and varied of vegetation. Certainly the millipede gave us a beautiful undulating track pattern, but it also showed us the first trails and runs we ever witnessed. In the larger animal world, the animals inhabit various areas that are strewn with intricate networks of roadways, highways, and byways. These roadways are called trails and runs and are quite easy to see and study, but just locating them was not enough for Grandfather. We missed many of the other smaller animal runs made by mice, voles, weasels, and numerous other small animals, and thus the millipede became another tracking teacher of profound proportion.

Because the millipedes live in the decaying vegetation, their little worlds are netted with vast, intricate roadways much like larger animal trails and runs. This tiny world of the millipede presents a magnificent challenge to even the most experienced tracker, but on a scale immediately accessible to the beginner.

Bush katydid (*Scudderia furcata*)

The bush katydid is an insect related to the true katydid, but differs in several respects. Unlike the true katydid that lives in trees, the bush katydid prefers to live in the bushes and hedgerows throughout the country. The width of their forewings is

Bush Katydid

uniform for the entire length, differing from the angular-winged katydid. The bush katydids lay flat eggs about a quarter-inch long in rows upon the leaves of the food tree in late summer. These hatch the following season and resemble the adults, except they are wingless. They generally eat the leaves of the plant on which they are found.

Rick and I used the katydid, like the cricket, for hearing tests. Depending on the weather, they can seem to be ventriloquists and are hard to find by hearing alone. To pinpoint their locations Rick and I would enter thickets and try to feel the vibrations of their voices as well as listen to the sounds.

Katydids are beautiful big insects, a joy to watch. It was one of the first insects I taught my son to know. His joy was to collect a few, place them in a terrarium for a few days and listen to their song indoors. He would release them after a few days because they did not make very good pets, some refusing to eat upon confinement.

They are a lesson in camouflage as well as sound deception in that they blend so beautifully with their surroundings.

Blister beetle (*Epicauta spp.*)

The blister beetle is one of the more common beetles of the hedgerows. There are over 200 kinds of blister beetles in the United States. Those most commonly encountered are about an inch long and are striped with red, yellow, and black; the wing covers are yellowish with two black stripes on each. Their bodies are very soft, cylindrical, and joined to the head by a distinctive, thick neck. They are found, mostly, on foliage and flowers of many types. Usually they are found upon the plants that they eat. You can find them at all levels of the hedgerow, depending on the plant species present.

Females lay their eggs in masses of over a hundred, in late summer or fall, usually very close to a grasshopper's egg capsule. The eggs hatch from twelve to twenty-four days into what is called a triungulin larvae, which will feed on the grasshopper's egg casing for several days. Over the next few weeks, a strange but beautiful metamorphosis occurs. They will then molt into caraboid larvae, which are less active. This is followed by two

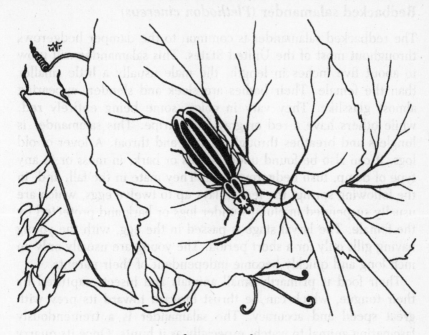

Blister Beetle

separate scarabaeidoid larval stages, each lasting a week. There is
a fifth (coarctate) larval stage, a sixth (scolytoid) larval stage,
and finally, a six-day pupal stage. Even in the immature stages,
because it feeds on a great number of other insects, this beetle
plays a vital role in maintaining the balances of insect populations.
As an adult, it transforms into a herbivore and feeds primarily on
plants. Blister beetles can secrete a protective stinging substance
that, if the substance is concentrated enough, can cause a severe
skin injury.

The blister beetle adult can be quite beautiful in appearance.
However, my favorite form of the blister beetles is the pre-adult
stage, because of their secretive, mystical, predatory behavior.
Their appetites then are voracious. Their approach to killing other
insects for food is very cunning, even though they look decep-
tively docile and harmless. Blister beetles know how to hide well
and are very difficult to see unless you know exactly what you are
looking for. You will probably come upon the blister beetle by
accident, and then the study is utterly fascinating.

Redbacked salamander (*Plethodon cinereus*)

The redbacked salamander is common to the damper hedgerows throughout most of the United States. This salamander will grow to about five inches in length, the male usually a little smaller than the female. Their bodies are sleek and slender, appearing almost glasslike. They vary in color, some being entirely red, while others have a red or gray back stripe. This salamander is lungless and breathes through its skin and throat. A lover of old logs, it can also be found under leaves or bark, in moss or in any type of damp, lush hedgerow trash. They mate in the fall, and, in the following spring, the female lays up to twelve eggs, which are usually suspended in clumps under logs or bark and protected by the female. The larval stage is passed in the egg, with the young having gills only for a short period. The young are usually only an inch long and quickly become independent of their parents.

Their food is primarily small animals and insects captured by their tongue, which can be thrust forward toward its prey with great speed and accuracy. The salamander is a tremendously fascinating animal to watch, especially as it hunts. Once its quarry is located, it will cautiously stalk to within the range of its tongue and snap the quarry up. The best time to see the salamanders is at dusk or dawn. In the daytime, they are less active and burrow deep within the very leafy and loamy hedgerow environment. With careful digging, however, they can be unearthed and studied. Be careful when handling these salamanders, as a dry hand could choke off their air supply. The redbacked salamander also has the ability to throw off a protective slime, and its tail will detach if grabbed.

Garter snake (*Thamnophis sirtalis*)

The garter snake is one of the most widely found reptiles in the United States. Though I've chosen to include it into the hedgerow chapter, it can live in any number of environments. Garter snakes blend well in, and become an important part of, the hedgerow's ecology. It can grow to thirty-six inches in length and is usually colored with a central light stripe down the middle of its back, bordered on each side by a dark stripe. Its sides are usually darker and its underparts usually lighter. Especially after the shedding of its skin, the garter snake's markings are clear, distinctive, and very beautiful. This, coupled with its movement through dappled sunny areas, creates the image that the snake has been highly oiled or waxed. When the sun strikes at the proper angle, it seems to glow with its own internal light.

Garter snakes will mate in early spring and in late summer. During spring mating season, when they are the most active, is the best time to see garter snakes. Ten to sixty young are born alive, each of them up to six inches long. Their diet includes salamanders, toads, frogs, earthworms, and insects of all types. I have known them to even eat small mice, though they prefer cold-blooded animals. Their bite is not poisonous, but they can strike quite viciously. When bothered or pursued by a predator, they will exude a vile smelling liquid, which probably makes them unpalatable.

The first snake that I ever encountered was probably the garter snake. Their way of movement and their ability to hunt are wondrous. It is almost a mystical experience to watch a garter snake stalking a toad or a salamander. It will approach slowly and

Garter snake

elegantly so as not to startle its quarry. It will coil slightly and then strike, injesting the animal headfirst.

Snakes have captured the imagination of people since the dawn of creation. Too often, they are considered evil, and people have taken to killing them without reason. With a little study, however, every snake, no matter how poisonous, can be understood and appreciated for its important role in the ecosystem. Snakes are an intricate link in the system of checks and balances nature has created for itself. We should not disrupt this delicate balance by allowing superstition to overshadow clear thinking. One of the delights in nature is watching the total picture and the intricate web of life connecting to all things. There is no greater teacher of this web of life than the snake.

Catbird (*Dumetella carolinensis*)

The catbird is a beautiful bird of our hedgerows, especially the thicker, overgrown areas that are teeming with insects. It is slate gray, with a black cap and a rusty-colored undertail. The tail appears large and broad when the bird is in flight, yet, when perched hangs loose and very long. The nest, located in dense shrubs anywhere from three to eight feet from the ground, appears bulky and deeply hollowed, made of woven twigs and bark, lined with leaves and small roots. Four to six eggs are laid. They are a deep, greenish blue and waxy in appearance. Incubation time is usually up to fourteen days and is done by both parents.

The food of the catbird in the spring is made up primarily of insects, mostly caterpillars, ants, and beetles. It is especially fond of gypsy moths. (Because the East has a problem with these moths, I try to encourage the nesting of catbirds whenever I can.) However, in summer and fall, they become more herbivores, seeking out fruits and other vegetable matter. Their distinctive call, almost a mewing, catlike sound, is very beautiful, standing out from the general bird symphony.

Whenever I think of a hedgerow, the voice of the catbird is always there. Its markings so intricately blend with the areas of light and shadow, its movements, though abrupt, seem so natural in the hedgerow tangles. I can picture them in my mind, dancing from twig to limb around tangles and across the leafy ground in a

Catbird

series of hops, darts, bobs, and short flights. Sometimes, when the conditions are right, its coloration causes it to appear as a puff of smoke drifting about brushscape.

White-eyed vireo (*Vireo griseus*)

The white-eyed vireo is a gorgeous bird with a wing spread of only about eight inches. One of the brighter inhabitants of our brush tangles and hedgerows, it is yellowish green, much like a patch of filtered sunlight, lighter underneath, with two conspicuous whitish wing bars, yellow sides and a whitish throat. The iris of its eye is white, and its bill is black. The yellow surrounding its eyes makes the vireo appear to sport spectacles.

The nests are built in low thickets and hedgerows, usually suspended from a fork in a shrub, anywhere from three to eight feet from the ground. It is cup-shaped and elegantly manufactured from interwoven grasses, moss, cobwebs, and sometimes lichens. The inner part of the nest is reserved for the finest and silkiest of linings. Usually four beautiful white eggs, barely speckled at the larger end with fine purplish or black spots, are laid in

White-eyed Vireo

the nest. It may take up to sixteen days for the brood to hatch. Both parents care for the nest and will defend it viciously, even to the point of self-sacrifice if need be.

The food of the white-eyed vireo is mostly insects, including caterpillars and ants, though it usually prefers to catch insects in flight around the hedgerow area. It will also eat berries.

The vireo is one of my favorite bursts of color in the hedgerow. Though the vireo is retiring and secretive, you can get close enough to it if you take your time and allow it to come to you. Approaching a vireo's nest is like walking into fire, considering the birds' very defensive behavior. It is best to sit by a large population of flying insects within the confines of the hedgerow and await the vireo's arrival. Despite their color, they can be very elusive and hard to spot, especially where the golden sun dappling is heaviest.

White-throated sparrow (*Zonotrichia albicollis*)

Slightly larger and chunkier than the white-eyed vireo is the white-throated sparrow, another familiar bird of our hedgerows.

It is a large member of the sparrow family, and is distinguished by black and white stripes on its crown, and a yellow band that runs horizontally between the bill and the eye. It also has a very clear white throat patch, which gives it its name. Females are duller in color and usually smaller than the male. (It is related to the white-crowned sparrow found in the western United States.) The song of the white-throated sparrow is one of the most beautiful of the spring bird songs and sounds much like "Drink you tea-tea-tea," or "Ol' Sam Peabody," depending on who you ask.

The white-throated sparrow nests in the confines of brushy thickets and hedgerows, though it can sometimes be found in damper areas. The nests are usually located on the ground or low in the brush, but rarely more than a foot above the ground. They are constructed of soft interwoven leaves and grasses, the finer grasses used for the inner lining. The eggs can be bluish, grayish, or greenish, with a spangle of dark-brown or black spots. The four or five eggs are incubated by the female for up to fourteen days; depending on the geographic location, two broods may be raised annually. This little bird hunts for its food on the hedgerow ground or scratches just below the surface in search of seeds and insects. It hops across the ground, digs with its bill, and scratches clownishly for its food. Generally, if you hear scratching from your hedgerow, it is probably a white-throated sparrow.

To me, the white-throated sparrows seem to have bright, buoyant trusting personalities. In all the hedgerows I have sat in, this is the bird that most consistently will approach within inches of where I sit, going about its daily business paying little attention to my presence. In fact, many times these little birds have landed on my shoulder or legs as they hopped across the ground in search of food. Whether or not a bird will approach often depends on either how *long* you have been still or how *still* you can become. With the white-throated sparrow, it is best to keep your movements slow and unthreatening. These birds are always a delight for children.

Chipmunk (*Tamias striatus*)

The chipmunk can live almost anywhere from the woodlands and brush tangles to the hedgerows of suburbia to parks of large urban areas. They blend in beautifully with the man-made environment and quickly become an intricate part to our suburban ecosystem. This little squirrel-like creature has brown or gray fur with five pronounced black stripes running along its back. Its underparts and lower cheeks are light tannish-red. Crossing the eye area is a distinctive dark streak with a white underline, and the throat is white.

There can be two litters a year—one in the spring from a fall breeding, and one in the fall from a spring breeding—of about five young per litter. Their food is a variety of plant and animal matter but consists primarily of nuts, fruit, and the seeds of wild plants. They are also known to eat baby birds, insects, and other small animals, though this seems to vary from chipmunk to chipmunk. Surprisingly certain chipmunks appear to develop a taste for baby birds while others will pass them up, and I have found that the birds know which chipmunks are dangerous to their young and which are not. Somehow, probably instinctively, the parent birds know the actions characteristic of a possibly predatory chipmunk. I have also found that some chipmunks will eat a certain kind of insect while others will not. The range of a chipmunk can be up to three acres, and it will periodically forage in the open areas of our lawns.

Chipmunks dig tunnels or burrows throughout their immediate home territory. Some of them are used for homes, while others are primarily for escape. Chipmunks are tamed very easily and will, within a few weeks, eat directly out of your hand. Grandfather could simply walk into my backyard, give a few chipping noises by pursing his lips, and have several chipmunks come to him. As he sat on the grass next to our hedgerow, they would climb onto his shoulders and work their way through his pockets, looking for hidden treats.

It is important to remember that, as with people, no two animals are alike. Each has its own special personality, slightly different than the rest of his kind. Only close, careful observation can define clearly variations in personality, habit, and even color and marking patterns. Once we learn that there are no two things alike (and I include plants), we find the continuous study of any one species ever changing, ever exciting and in no way boring. These subtle differences and the multitude of variation make life's wonders rich and full.

ABANDONED AREAS

Beyond the manicured lawns and tidy hedgerows that separate the houses that make up our suburbia, there is an even more diverse world of nature. The abandoned lots, old fields, roadsides, brush tangles, and isolated forest stands that dot almost all our communities—there for anyone who will venture beyond the yard limits—are bountiful islands of the natural world, havens for all manner of beast and leaf, a footnote of what once was. Indeed, for anyone entering one of these abandoned areas for the first time, the experience can be quite a shock. Here, one can blot out the sounds of civilization, step back in time and place and see, firsthand, what an area once looked like before it was developed. Without venturing very far, one can experience the purity of the natural world, capturing adventures as great as any to be found in our wilderness areas. By far, in our communities these abandoned areas of the suburban wilderness afford the best opportunity for study and the greatest variety of fauna and flora.

These fringe areas of our communities can be divided into a number of different and diverse areas, each hosting its own unique population. Though the areas are different by nature, the animals will utilize all adjacent areas for their livelihood, making sharp boundaries impossible. In these areas people don't expect to find the abundance of wildlife and the diversity of plants existing so close to the sea of houses and roadways they call civilization. A pile of junk dumped in these areas may become an eyesore, but with time and plant growth they turn into a makeshift rock-cavern jungle, homes to all manner of beast. Nature tries to fill every unpolluted niche, and it is in these niches that we can find the joy of pure nature.

ABANDONED LOTS, OLD FIELDS, AND ROADSIDES

These lots, fields, and unmanicured roadsides are usually found at various locations throughout, or just outside, our communities—a building lot long abandoned and not yet purchased, a junk-car graveyard no longer in use, or perhaps a strip of land along the road leading out of the town proper. Throughout these areas runs a network of pathways, similar in layout to our most intricate systems of highways, byways, and back roads, on which the drama of survival, the life and death struggle, takes place daily. It is here that a wide variety of animals and plants can be found. It is to here that we can drift at any time of the day to study, to understand, and to enjoy the wild beauty.

The night's curtain pulls back slowly, revealing a golden dawn that bedazzles the damp grasses. Bird voices, few and uncertain at first, increase to a grand song, soon joined by the voice and wing of the myriad insects. The grasses and weeds literally vibrate with the sound and motion of animals going about their morning activities. The landscape seems at once alive, far removed from the stirrings of the civilized world just outside its boundaries, and not yet awake. At first the birds are the most active as they go about the daily business of feeding, nest building, or defending their territories. Their activity assaults the senses.

As the dew dries from the grasses, the birds' exuberant activity drops off a bit and their voices fade to a low pervasive hum. Soon the insects shake the chill from their shells and begin their song. All around is the sound of tiny wings and chirping calls. The grasshoppers begin their song as if following a classic curve, rising and falling in tone and intensity. Other insects join in chorus and, with the birds, create a symphony of sound and motion so full it rocks the soul.

Beneath the sea of grasses and under the matting of tangled

dead grass cover are the tunnels and roadways of the voles. These tiny rodents are one of the most numerous mammals of these old lots, fields, and roadsides, making up a large percentage of the predators' diets. Everywhere in the inner recesses of the grasses, the voles are living out their lives, raising families, feeding, creating new tunnels, or hiding from enemies. Weasels, shrews, and mice run these vole roadways on their hunting or foraging excursions. At this time of the morning, most of these little mammals are on their way back to their homes, to retire after a long night's hunt. Their homes can be found in the grasses, in small herbal tangles, or under old boards and other garbage discarded by society.

Voles live in the interface of earth and leaf. Their tunnels wind through the "grass-scape" in intricate patterns. By carefully pulling back the grasses and looking at the bases, you can discover this network of roadways, bedding areas, feeding areas, and denning areas. I often lose myself for hours, in some cases days, exploring these vole cities. Many times when I am on a book tour or awaiting transportation, I occupy my free time by visiting these fringe areas. The animal and plant magic is as beautiful and wondrous as in any of the wilderness areas. When your head is down looking at these little towns, except for the noise of civilization, it is the same as in any wilderness area.

One of the best places an outdoors person can practice tracking is in these vole cities. The grasslands are littered with all types of animal signs. Trails, runs, escape areas, feeding and bedding areas, hair, scratchings, gnawings, scat, rubs, and many other signs are there for the close observer's scrutiny. Dealing with animal signs on such a small level makes the tracker a better sign reader, for these areas push the observation skills to the limit. Voles are also very important to the overall ecosystem, not only because they are so prolific and on the diet of most predators, but also because where there are voles, you will find many other animals. Voles are an indicator animal, meaning that when they are there, the food supply and conditions are favorable for all manner of mice, weasels, shrews, chipmunks, rabbits, and many other animals, including most medium-size predators.

It is possible, even near dense populations of people, to see some of the larger predators hunting these abandoned lots and fields, and even along our roadsides. In the early morning or at dusk, if you sit quietly by the edge of these areas, you may get a glimpse of a fox or coyote or owl or hawk. In many parts of the country it would not be unusual to see skunks, raccoons, opossums, rabbits, and all manner of other medium-size animals, both predator and prey alike. If these fringe areas of grassland are near stands of forest, you are also likely to see deer, and other large mammals, foraging for food. The succulents in these areas draw animals from all around.

It is good to keep in mind that the animals of the fringe areas, especially the medium to larger mammals and birds, are quite used to life among civilization. They have adapted ways to move within this realm undetected, by even the more experienced observers. As a rule of thumb, I expect the unexpected when observing animals near civilization. Their habits can vary slightly to dramatically from that of their wilderness counterparts, and special steps must be taken in order to observe an animal in this setting.

As a prime example of the unexpected, I offer the day I discovered a way that a small group of deer made their way into an abandoned field that was virtually surrounded by houses. I had expected the animals to come from the south, along a thin strip of forest that bordered a school yard. I thought that this approach would be the best for deer since the school yard was abandoned at night and they were relatively safe from sightings by nearby neighbors. My theory was logical, though upon inspection of the tree line, I found no place for the deer to bed down and no regular deer tracks along the pathways.

I sat for a number of nights watching these animals for hours. Each time, they would suddenly, mystically disappear just before dawn. They seemed to vanish into the mists at the far end of the field. I was on a speaking tour at the time, and the fields were heavily posted with No Trespassing signs. On the last night in the area, my curiosity got the best of me, so I camouflaged myself and headed to the far end of the field that was bordered by houses. Using a small flashlight, but mostly by feel, I followed the deer tracks only to find, to my amazement, that they had disappeared into the wall of a train trestle, using a small drain tube. I crouched down and crawled through the tube for several yards and ended up behind an abandoned warehouse. Several acres of thick brush and low, dense vegetation grew, housing the deer in complete safety. At the far end of the warehouse, the farmlands began, and the deer had access to the best of both worlds.

BRUSH TANGLES AND CLOSED FORESTS

Wilder and thicker than the hedgerows are the closed forests and brush tangles of our suburban wildernesses. Typically these areas are surrounded by developments or factories, creating islands that range from less than an acre to many acres. These larger wilder places become the refuge of many of the animals that frequent our grasslands, lawns, and hedgerows. Any brush tangle and closed forest with a nearby grassy field provides an excellent habitat for many of the wilder and more elusive animals. These areas in our communities should be protected in their natural state and not cultivated into a manicured park.

The brush tangles and closed forests are wilder than the hedgerows, containing many animals that you would not expect to see outside of the true wilderness. Because you don't expect to see them, you may never look, and thus they go unnoticed. It only takes a young boy or girl with the curiosity of the natural world to find these animals, much to the disbelief of parents and communities. These areas afford a tremendous opportunity for study, when you can't go to the wilderness. And let's face it, in our workaday world, there is little chance of going far from our communities, especially during the weekdays. But that is no reason to let our awareness skills slide. During the morning hour before work or school, or during the evening, is the best time to study these miniature stands of wilderness.

These enclaves of nature begin to stir at first light, usually a long time before the day gets going in our civilized world. Animals in these areas modify their natural habits in order to blend in and go undetected. You will find their habits and food just slightly different from their wilder counterparts, but the dawn and dusk still hold the greatest promise for your study. Many of my students who live in communities make a semipermanent blind in the wild places of their neighborhood, thus the local animal populations get used to the presence of the structure and eventually pay it little attention. Some of the greatest wildlife shots I've seen have been shot just on the outskirts of a town or development.

The dawn mist shrouds the blend of forest and brush, making it appear as if in a dream. Almost out of focus, like a huge wall, are the house rows that border the area on two sides. Within the confines of this jungle come the faint stirrings and calls of animals as they finish their night of foraging. A raccoon slowly ambles up a tree to a large cavity it calls home. It has eaten well, an even blend of natural food and scraps from the garbage cans. There in this hollow oak it makes its permanent home, above all the trials and danger of the daylight hours. No one ever seems to take notice of its home, high off the ground and obscured by limbs and vines.

In another corner of the forest an opossum also crawls into its home, a hollow branch of a large willow that had broken but not fallen in a storm many years ago. It was born in this tree and now is the last living member of its original family. Most of the others were killed by dogs and cars. It was a bit smarter than its brothers and sisters and learned to survive within the limits of its environment. It now nursed a brood that clung to its fur. One of the young died during the night's forage when it wandered off and got caught by a large neighborhood tomcat. It is rare that this will happen, because the young do not wander far from their mother during this stage of their development, but this is the law of survival and only those that learn the rules will survive.

At the outer edge of the forest, in the thick tangles of brush, a red fox wraps its tail around its body and quietly sleeps. Its home is not in a hollow or a hole but on the ground, secure in a brush tangle. It also has returned from a night of hunting the grasslands and brush. Its greatest kill was a young pheasant that had strayed in from an adjacent field near an old farm. Its night's hunt had led it many miles, in and out of the sea of houses, along hedgerows, through thickets, over abandoned lots and fields, and into the little forests. Secretly it went about its business, disturbing nothing, carefully avoiding all contact with man and dogs. This was its fifth year and it was an admirable master of deception, camouflage, and stalking—well in control of the terrors of the unnatural world that lay only a few hundred yards behind it.

A skunk also finished its foraging as it ripped apart the earth surrounding an old rotted log. It would retire into the recesses of an old pile of cinder blocks that created a natural cave. The tops of the blocks were overgrown with poison ivy and other vegetation, including bull brier, which made the skunk's home impenetrable to man or dog. Here it was safe and secure from everything. Its home well chosen, though not entirely natural, it lived safe and secure from all enemies. Its backup defenses are its powerful scent glands, as well as a learned ability to escape detection and live within the confines of this civilization and the surrounding islands of nature.

Here also are the long-tailed weasels, chipmunks, white-footed mice, voles, and numerous birds and insects. The trees are a natural haven for cicadas and katydids, as well as all manner of caterpillar and insect. During the daylight hours the cicadas add to the sounds of grasshoppers, birds, and other insects to create a grand chorus. At night the cicadas blend with the crickets to create a more subtle but stimulating symphony. Always the trees and brush are in song and motion, creating a symphony of sound and flow that literally rocks the spirit and adds a touch of nature to the surrounding community. One cannot sit by any of these areas without being overwhelmed by the variety of life that is all around. The person who sits and waits with a certain patience and dedication will be rewarded far beyond his or her wildest dreams.

Here in the brush and trees is an assortment of warblers, sparrows, blackbirds, bluebirds, finches, verios, flycatchers, phoebes, and numerous other birds. They search from the upper branches of the trees to the forest floor. Everywhere is the motion of birds foraging, calling, singing, nest building, and flitting about. Some are delightfully colored, others are well camouflaged and blend in beautifully with the landscape. Everywhere you look and listen you will find the birds of these pockets of wilderness. Because of the islandlike nature and compactness of these forests, they will make good birding areas. You might see more species of birds in these areas than you would during the same time in a wilderness area. Habitat is scarce and the birds are more cramped together, thus you will not have far to travel.

In a small community just outside Pittsburgh I helped a former student construct a blind of old burlap sacks. With dead sticks, we built a frame about eight-foot long, six-foot wide and five-foot high. We covered the entire structure with burlap, throwing leaves and brush overall, just like a debris hut. We left six small windows and made the door toward a thick area that would cover our approach. We put comfortable benches inside, then abandoned the structure for a week. Our first morning and evening in the blind produced a phenomenal amount of animals. Even though the forest, field, and brush tangles were only twenty acres and were surrounded by houses, a school, and a factory, we saw more animals than we had on the same type of day in a wilderness area where we had held classes the week before. Now my student uses the blind as a place to sit and relax before and after work. The sightings, and possibilities for photographs, of the animals found in this small forest island boggles the imagination, yet most people do not realize the animals are there.

ANIMAL LIFE

Voles (*Microtus pennsylvanicus*)

Certainly, the untamed grasslands found along our roadways, abandoned lots, and old fields are the best suitable environments for the voles. Although the vole is despised by most farmers, orchardmen, and gardeners, it was a valuable first lesson for me in tracking. When Grandfather introduced me to the voles and the tiny vole cities, he thus introduced me to the realm of sign tracking, by which I learned to read telltale clues of animals.

My first encounter with the vole was a multileveled lesson. It was not only a lesson in tracking and observation but also in the variety of animals that a landscape could hold. Rick and I had always assumed that we had to get back to the woods to find the splendors of the natural world. But here in our first lesson in sign tracking, Grandfather showed us how nature fills every niche.

We were just beginning to learn the various signs of animals by picking telltale hair and scat from the landscape as well as locating many of the larger animal roadways. Grandfather excited us one day when he told us that he was going to take us to a very beautiful animal area that was so filled with animals that we would scarcely be able to count them all. He then led us quite a few miles from our home, along the major back roads and finally onto

Vole

a state highway. It was there at the edge of this busy roadway,
along the unkept thick fringe of grass that bordered its outskirts,
that we were introduced to the vole. Here, stretching before us
in myriad roadways, was a huge vole city; also it comprised less
than two acres of overall land. In the small patch that we searched,
which was no more than twenty-foot long by six-foot wide, we
found more than twenty-five voles, their bounded bedding areas,
feeding areas, roadway areas, and numerous other signs.

Not only did we learn from tracking the vole to look closely to
the ground and hone our observation skills to the point of picking
up fine detail, but also we learned of one of the most preyed upon
and prolific animals of the countryside. Grandfather, in his unique
way, was also making a statement, showing us that wild nature
could be found anywhere, even along some of the busiest highways in the state. We were in such awe that day—not only with
the newly discovered wildlife, but also with a handful of new
plants that we had never before seen, as well as the beauty and
intricacy of animal roadway design.

The vole is what I call the Volkswagen of the mouse world. At rest the vole's very rounded head, ears, and body, and the small eyes and tail, appear to have the outline of an old Volkswagen beetle. Voles (more commonly called meadow mice) can grow to 6½ inches with about a 1½ to 2-inch tail. Both sexes are colored alike. In the winter, they are grayish. In summer, however, they turn a chestnut brown with just a light dusting of black, the underside a bit grayer and sometimes dusted with just a touch of cinnamon. The young tend to be a lot darker.

Voles can be found throughout the U.S. They are a very prolific animal and a basic food of most predators. The female of the species, which has an average life span of one and a half years, can produce up to twelve litters a year, each litter containing four to eight young. The original litter is weaned in about ten days, and the mother can then breed again. Young females can breed at four weeks old and young males, after about a month and a half.

The vole has a voracious appetite, having to eat at least its own weight each day. It is active day and night throughout the year and will girdle trees and eat garden vegetables and vast grain crops. Ironically, in some areas the vole is so numerous that it has become a major competitor of domestic animals for forage. One good acre of grassland can support about 400 voles, but excellent areas can support populations of over 10,000 per acre. They do have a storage instinct, and their caches are easily located along the trails of their feeding areas.

White-footed mouse (*Peromyscus leucopus*)

One of my favorite mice people is the white-footed mouse. To me, they are not only the cutest of all mice, but their antics are also the most comical. They seem to be always at play, inquisitive, and very active. My first experience with the white-footed mouse was at the first debris hut I ever built in a survival situation. Rick and I had learned to build a debris hut one weekend, abandoned it, and returned the following weekend to live in it. Sometime between the building of the hut and its use, two white-footed mice took up residence in the upper rafters. During the weekend in the hut, they became quite friendly, to the point of taking scraps of food directly from our hands—though they stole quite a bit more from our larders. They were tamed

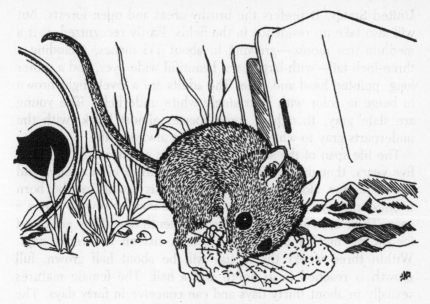

White-footed Mouse

easily and were always waiting in the debris hut whenever we returned.

In close proximity to the debris hut, we began construction on what we called the Good Medicine Cabin, a sturdy structure with a fireplace. The mice, which had grown in number because of a recent litter, watched from the nearby debris hut with great interest as our structure grew over the weeks. When Rick and I finally moved into the cabin and lit our first fire, the mice soon followed. Over the next several years, generation after generation of white-footed mice adopted our cabin as a home. Each mouse eventually had a name and we could easily tell them apart by their distinctive markings, including scars and freckles. Over the years these mouse companions proved helpful in honing our tracking skills, laying down tracks at the dusty entrance for our study. I grew very fond of their playful antics and lovable nature. As a word of caution, however, their bite can be very nasty.

The white-footed mouse can adapt to a variety of habitats, and can, in one species or another, be found throughout most of the

United States. It prefers the brushy areas and open forests, but will also take up residence in the fields. Easily recognized, it is a medium-size mouse—growing to about 7½ inches, including a three-inch tail—with large ears, beautiful wide eyes, and a rather long, pointed head and nose. The adults are a lovely light brown to beige in color with a strikingly white underbelly. The young are slate gray, though in some species almost black, with the underparts gray to white. Their feet are always white.

The life span of the white-footed mouse can normally be up to five years, though "Old Three-toes," who lived in our cabin, did live to a ripe old age of six. Three to six young can be born twenty-one days after breeding and there may be several litters a year. Their eyes are open on the eighteenth day. They are cared for by the mother and are weaned in sixteen to twenty days. Within three weeks the mouse will be about half grown; full growth is reached in a month and a half. The female matures sexually in about thirty days and can conceive in forty days. The male matures at about fifty days. White-footed mice are considered old at three years.

These mice consume both plant and animal matter, eating considerable quantities of insects, nuts, seeds, and plant shoots. They will also store plant matter for later use. They build beautiful houses of plant materials by capping and remodeling abandoned birds' nests, though they can be found in a treehole, under a log or board, or even in the house.

Long-tailed weasel (*Mustela frenata*)

The weasel is a cunning, silent, and deadly killer. It is probably one of the most aware of all hunters. Grandfather had such high respect for the weasel and its abilities that he would have us watch the ways of the hunting weasel and try to duplicate its movements through role-playing. The weasel quickly became, to us, as to the Native Americans, a living symbol of the hunt. Sleek and quick, they seem to flow over the landscape observing all movement, sound, sight, and smell. Nothing is overlooked, nothing is left to chance.

While visiting a friend in a well-developed area of northern

Weasel

New Jersey, I observed a weasel hunting along a hedgerow and in a nearby overgrown patch of grass. The weasel's presence was something of a surprise since we were in the midst of a rather large neighborhood barbecue. The weasel was threading its way along the hedgerow, unobserved by people or even the cat that lay at the junction between hedgerow and grass patch. It slipped so silently by the cat that the cat never turned or noticed that anything had passed inches from its tail. I had often seen weasels in the brush thickets surrounding my childhood home, but I hadn't expected them to blend so easily with humans and to gear their habits to become almost invisible to the cats and dogs. Since the sighting at the barbecue, I've observed many more weasels hunting in very suburban environments.

The weasel can be found anywhere from heavily populated neighborhoods to the roadsides of busy superhighways to abandoned wood lots. It is a master of deception, however, and its abilities to camouflage, hide, and stalk make it one of the harder animals to spot in a suburban environment. The best place to observe weasels is at the interface of a brush tangle or forest and grassland. Because the vole is a favorite prey of the weasel, vole trails widened by stalking weasels are sure indicators of a weasel's hunting pattern. By concealing yourself close to a weasel's run, you can easily spot the animal as it slips from the forest to the brushland at dusk or back again at dawn.

I often think that the weasel, when it is living so close to man, is a bit brazen, perhaps a bit foolhardy. That it can hunt with such ease at such close proximity is, I think, a sad statement about man's general level of awareness—an opinion obviously shared by the weasel. This doesn't say much for civilization's dog and cat population, either. You can, however, use the weasel's brazen attitude against it if you learn to pay close, and patient, attention to the hedgerows and overgrown places that surround your home. Apparently, the last thing a weasel expects is for a man to be hiding and observing it, and it will usually pay little attention to man's whereabouts, other than to circumnavigate him.

The long-tailed weasel grows to about seventeen inches in length, with a tail of about six inches. The female is slightly smaller, growing to only about fifteen inches. The weasel has a long slender body a neck longer than most mammals and a head that is only slightly larger than the neck. It has a brown coat, a beautiful yellow-white underpart and a black tip at the end of the tail. In the Northern climates, it becomes white in the winter but still sports the black tip at the tail's end. In the Southwest, the head is slightly darker than the body, with an off-white mask across the face.

The long-tailed weasel is the most widely distributed weasel in the United States, Canada, and Mexico, and can be found in virtually any habitat, especially near water. The adults mate in early summer and the young are born in midseason the following spring. The females can mate as early as at four weeks of age; the males, at about nine months to a year. Though they can climb trees and swim, they are not very good at either, unlike their otter cousins. Their diet consists mainly of voles and other rodents but they will take birds and some insects whenever the opportunity arises.

Red Fox

Red fox (*Vulpes fulva*)

The red fox, like the long-tailed weasel, is a superb hunter and stalker, and is very elusive. It can easily live, completely undetected by man, on the edges of our suburban areas. As long as there are brush tangles, closed forests, and abandoned fields, there are homes enough for our fox brother. Their secretive behavior adds to their mystery and mystique. To me, they are the symbol of what the Apache scout stood for. Their ability to move silently and unseen was studied and emulated by the native peoples.

When Rick and I were very young, Grandfather instructed us to study the fox closely, to note the sense of effortless movement that made it appear as if the fox were floating through the forest and fields. Then we would mimic the fox walk, trying with all our concentration to move with the same effortless silence. Following the fox on its hunting circuit can be an awe-inspiring adventure. Like a ghost, it will slip through the underbrush, peek out through the early dawn mist and disappear into the dusk. Sometimes I would think I had imagined it, that it was simply a mirage. Sometimes it will travel where you least expect it. Rick and I were constantly being surprised, as it would pop into view, only to vanish the next moment. The fox is always a source of great excitement and adventure, and every encounter should be a cherished moment.

The foxes that live near our civilization are more secretive and cautious than those found in the wild. When I do spot them, despite their stealth and ability to camouflage, I'm often rather overcome by a sense of wonder—and respect. I've seen them hunt along backyard hedgerows that were buttressed on all sides by houses. Their trails and runs would wind around the houses where they afforded the best cover and yielded the best view. And on their feeding rounds they were so silent that they didn't even alarm the neighborhood dogs. At first light, the fox will usually abandon its hunting area and retire into the closed forest and brush tangles that lie just outside our suburban confines.

The best places to see foxes are at the edges of fields bordered by brush tangles and forests. From the edge cover, they'll slip into the fields and sit listening, as if to the grasses, waiting for the slightest movement or softest rustle that indicates a rodent or rabbit is passing. They'll stalk toward the disturbance, then pounce. Smaller rodents are eaten whole and larger rabbits are torn apart. When tracking the fox, one will often see deposited in the scat bits of the hair, bones, teeth, claws, whiskers, and skulls of the rodents, and insects, it has eaten. It is common also to find seeds in the scat, because the fox will sometimes eat fruits. The most important thing to keep in mind however is that foxes will be found in those parts of civilization where you least expect them.

The fox grows to about forty inches, which includes a six-inch bushy, black-tipped tail, and will weigh up to fifteen pounds. The body is quite sleek, with large pointed ears and a pointed nose. The males are larger than the females. The overall color is a reddish or a golden brown above, with white beneath and black legs. Young foxes have blackish muzzles and black on the back of the ears. Mating takes place from January to late February, and four to ten young, depending on the availability of food, will be born about fifty days later. Foxes will use converted groundhog burrows, hollow logs, rock outcroppings, and even garbage piles as shelters in which to raise their young. The mother and young foxes are fed by the male until the young leave home at about five months. They are full grown at about eighteen months. Foxes can live up to fourteen years, but the average life span is half that.

The best territory for foxes is mixed cover, especially wooded areas bordering farmlands. They are found throughout the United States, with few territorial exceptions. Their food consists of mice, carrion, fruit and vegetables, and game, but the largest portion of the diet is rodents. The fox has a great sense of smell, excellent hearing, and good eyesight. It is tremendously intelligent and is known for its endurance. They are active year-round, usually at night, but can be seen in the daytime. The fox does not climb trees like its gray fox cousin.

Opossum (*Didelphis marsupialis*)

Depending on the area, the opossum can grow to a remarkable size in both weight and length. The average length is about forty inches with an eighteen-inch tail. Opossum tails are ratlike and virtually hairless in appearance, but are prehensile (meaning that they can grasp and hold with their tails). Sometimes you'll find them hanging from the trees, the entire body suspended from just the tail. The ears of the opossum also lack hair. The feet are black, but the rest of the furred body is a grayish white. The eyes are very large and dark—a striking contrast to the white face.

The opposum is quite active year-round, especially at night. It is not, however, a very skilled hunter, being rather slow, but, in defense, it may threaten to fight, or take a feeble bite, but most often it will play dead. It lives in the wooded areas and brush tangles in hollow trees and other cavities, preferably off the ground and often pretty dirty. These dens are usually located quite close to their food source. The opossum will eat almost anything organic; eggs are a particular favorite.

Because the opossum is marsupial (North America's only), the young—up to twenty, and born about two weeks after mating— upon birth make their way up to their mother's pouch, where they attach themselves to one of the teats and nurse for about two months. At about four weeks, the young will begin to stick their

Opossum

heads outside the pouch, and at about five weeks they will leave
the pouch temporarily at intervals. After about eight weeks, the
young opossum forages for itself. Opossums can live eight years or
more and are capable of breeding one year after birth.

The opossum was one of the first animals I stalked up to and
touched. Rick and I, figuring that they were very slow and not as
aware as many other animals, assumed they would be an easy
mark. When Grandfather first introduced us to stalking, we practiced the slow flowing motion, ultimately touching all manner of
insects, frogs, and turtles, but the opossum was the first mammal
we stalked and touched. We had heard the stories about opossums playing dead when confronted, so, even with their ominous-
looking teeth, we felt that it was a safe animal to touch.

Slipping nimbly through the brush and careful not to crack a
twig, we stalked up to our first opossum, which was feeding near
a fallen log. We edged our bodies within inches of the log, where
the opossum kept feeding, taking no notice of our presence. I was
the closest, so it was our plan that I would softly touch it first, and
Rick would get the second touch. I slowly edged my hand over

the log and touched it gently on its side, at which point all hell broke loose. Instead of the opossum playing dead, it charged at my hand with its mouth wide open. I quickly withdrew my hand with a yell and the opossum proceeded to charge over the log, run right down Rick's back, and disappear into the brush.

From then on, no matter how docile we thought an animal would be, we always approached it and touched it with the utmost caution. With carnivores and omnivores, it is best to touch them without them knowing. Even some of the most docile birds can inflict wounds to the hands and face if you are not careful.

Meadowlark (*Sturnella magna*)

The eastern meadowlark grows to eleven inches in length and has a wingspread of about eighteen inches. The female is much smaller than the male. The birds are stout and sport a stubby tail with white outer feathers. It has a distinctive black bib line and a yellow breast and throat. The overall coloration is light brown, loosely speckled with darker brown. The meadowlark nests on the ground, using dried grasses as the primary building material. The nest is usually camouflaged in a thick growth of growing grasses so that, at first appearance, it looks very much like a tunnel in the grass. Some of these nests will have two separate openings. The inner part of the nest is usually lined with finer materials, softer grasses, bits of down. The meadowlarks can lay up to six eggs, which are whitish and speckled with either brown or deep purple. The female does all the incubation. Meadowlarks' home territory, which they will defend quite vigorously, usually extends over several acres. During the summer months, the meadowlark feeds mainly on insects of all types, but as winter approaches, and insect population dwindles, they will also eat wild seeds. The song of the Eastern meadowlark is a distinctive series of precise whistles, while the Western meadowlark has more of a warbling song. No matter what the species, however, Eastern or Western, the song is clear, distinct, and beautiful.

Every time I hear the meadowlark song, it brings back images painful and beautiful. The window of my third-grade classroom looked out over a large grass field. During the spring of one year, a pair of nesting meadowlarks set up their home close—much too

Meadowlark

close in my teacher's opinion—to the classroom. Their songs and antics were so captivating that I would drift off for long periods listening and watching instead of paying attention to the lesson at hand. Many days I stayed after school as punishment for "daydreaming." For the life of me, I could not make my teacher understand that I was watching the meadowlarks, nor did she seem to care. But during my lunch hour and break time, I would go outside and watch the meadowlarks raising their young and savor their songs. To me, a field without a meadowlark song is hardly a field at all, for the meadowlark adds a beauty and intrigue that cannot be replaced.

Locating a meadowlark's nest can be quite an undertaking, as Rick and I once discovered after spending two days watching a female meadowlark at the far end of a field. Meadowlarks are somewhat sly when entering and exiting their nests, so that predators will have a hard time discovering them. If a meadowlark suspects that it is being watched, it will drop to the ground near the nest, then weave its way through to the actual nest site.

They are so quiet, and devious, in their flight that they could be flying along one moment and then seemingly vanish as if into thin air the next. It took Rick and I quite a few days to narrow down ten acres of field to twenty square feet, but we were still unable to find the nest. Nevertheless, the exercise made us careful observers.

Grasshopper sparrow (*Ammodramus savannarum*)

The grasshopper sparrow is a smaller sparrow than many of the other sparrow species. It measures a little over five inches long and has about an eight-inch wingspan. The female is much smaller than the male. Both sexes are colored alike, with an unstreaked breast, though the young birds have streaked breasts, and a very short stumpy tail. This sparrow can be found in grasslands throughout much of the United States.

The nesting habits of the grasshopper sparrow are similar to those of the meadowlark. Nests are built in open fields, on the ground, and are sometimes sunken with the surface grass-covered, so as to be virtually undetectable. The inside of the nest can be lined with hair, roots, or other soft, downy plant matter. The eggs are glossy, vary in color from white to greenish, and are lightly spotted with purple or brown speckles. Both sexes help incubate the young. The grasshopper sparrow runs through the grasses over well-defined trail systems in its search for insects, caterpillars, ants, spiders, and other such invertebrates. Weed seeds comprise a small part of their overall diet. Their song is very faint and insectlike, almost like a buzzing or a whirring. The young will follow the adults through their foraging runs for quite some time.

The grasshopper sparrow is a secretive little bird that slips through its grassland environment so deftly that it is almost invisible. It takes a keen eye to pick them out, unless, of course, you catch sight of one in flight. My first encounter with the grasshopper sparrow was much by accident. Rick and I were walking across an open field just outside the school playground area when we came upon a wounded sparrow. It hobbled along in front of us, drooping a wing now and then, and as we tried to get closer, it would fly off perfectly healthy only to resume the activity. Greatly puzzled by the bird's behavior, we noted the field markings of the bird and went to the school library to learn what we could. We identified it as a grasshopper sparrow and discovered that one of its habits to lure predators away from its nest was to feign injury.

The next day, we headed out to the same location and again the injured bird appeared. This time we did not follow, but carefully, on our hands and knees, began to look for the nest. Though the general area surrounding the nest could not have been more than a hundred square feet, it took us nearly two hours to locate it. The entire time, the mother bird kept trying to lure us away. The nest was so well hidden that I have doubts that most predators, even walking right by it, would have found it, unless, of course, they had a keen sense of smell. Over the period of that spring, the sparrows grew accustomed to our visits. They stopped feigning injury and would proceed with their daily business. We would sit for hours watching the parents, whose markings beautifully blended with the environment, slip in and out of the grasses and pluck insects from the lower grasses and ground. The grasshopper sparrow is truly one of the masters of camouflage.

Meadow grasshopper (*Orchelium vulgare*)

The meadow grasshopper is a lover of moist pastures and meadows, and prefers to live among the grassy plants. From tip of the head to the tip of the wing it is, in overall length, only a little more than two inches. Its body is slender and its head sports two very long, threadlike antennae. It is a beautiful pale green in color, with dark eyes located very close to the front of the head. Unlike some grasshoppers, the meadow grasshopper stays very close to the ground. Its eggs are laid on plant leaves and hatch in the spring. The young resemble the adults but do not develop wings until maturity. They feed mostly on grasses. On the male the left front wing overlaps the right in order to produce the distinctive grasshopper clicking call. Beneath the wings are scrapers that produce the vibrating raspy sound so commonly heard in our grasslands and waste places.

Many times Rick and I would collect animals, study them for a

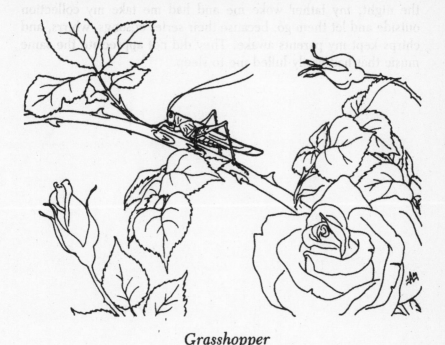

Grasshopper

few days and release them again in their original habitats. Though I do not believe in the prolonged captivity of any animal, I feel that keeping an insect or other small animal for a few days in a suitable terrarium can give us great insights into its life habits. It is important to keep in mind, however, that captivity will produce some deviation in an animal's normal routine. No animal, including insects, should be kept in a jar, but rather should be kept in a big airy terrarium with a topography that's designed to resemble closely the animal's natural habitat. And never for more than a day or two.

The best time to collect insects, especially ones that move quite fast and escape easily, is at dawn. The insects are chilled from the night's air and will usually lie quite dormant on the grasses and foliage until the air or sunlight warms them to activity. Once I had, at one time, two green frogs, an assortment of katydids, cicadas, crickets and grasshoppers in my room. Halfway through the night, my father woke me and had me take my collection outside and let them go, because their series of songs, whirrs, and chirps kept my parents awake. They did not appreciate the same music that had easily lulled me to sleep.

PONDS, STREAMS, AND DRAINAGE DITCHES

The suburban areas that often support the most wildlife, and by far my favorite areas, are the water systems that run through our communities. I am particularly fond of the ponds and swamps. For me, water has a magical quality that not only draws animals but also humans. Here the wildlife abundance is remarkable, the life-and-death struggle more pronounced, and the ease with which an attentive tracker can spot animals far better than in many wilder areas. Water is the heart of any area since any number of animals from the surrounding wild areas make their daily mecca to these sources of life. To the ancients, water was Earth Mother's blood; a few hours sitting by any of these damp areas will show you why.

Morning activity at the pond starts at first light. Insect songs of the night will soon give way to bird and insect songs of the day. Frogs have been quiet for a few hours now and insects slowly trail off in sound as the chill of the night settles in and quietens their songs. Momentarily, there is almost a complete silence in the air as the night sounds wane and the day sounds have not yet begun. If you sit back and relax, concealed by the brush, you can almost feel a pulse coming from deep within the swamp. There is an anticipation, an excitement in the air, as if all the animals are waiting for the right moment to begin their stirrings and songs. One can't help but get caught up in this anticipation. You find yourself waiting, as if you were on the edge of your seat, for the initial downbeat of the conductor's baton.

83

At first it may be a lone bird, calling nervously now and then, as if testing the predawn air. Another bird voice joins the first—this one a little less nervous—then another, then another, then another, until the air vibrates with a rich symphony of birdsong. As the first rays of sun strike the vegetation and the insects warm, their voices and vibrating wings are added to the overall symphony. Though not as intensely as in last night's song, the frogs may chime in, but not for very long. This song is joined by the splash of fish and the rustle of animals, the day becomes a beautiful blend of music throughout the pond.

In the pond's waters, stir the sunfish that nibble on all manner of insects and vegetation. The large bass cruise around, watching for an unsuspecting fish, insect, or frog to become their meal. Smaller fish hug the pond weed and banks for protection, camouflage, and escape. They, too, are looking for insects and the young of many aquatic animals. Many types of frogs—green, bullfrog, leopard, and pickerel—sun themselves or, half submerged in the water, wait for insects. Insect larvae, tadpoles, fish fry, and innumerable other small beasts turn the pond waters into a sort of biological soup. Fishing spiders, water snakes, water striders, and back swimmers make up a large part of the population and add to the overall splendor of this wild place.

Weasel tracks are found along the bank, intermixed with raccoon prints that show where the animals foraged for some freshwater clams and crayfish. The raccoon lives in a nearby hollow tree in a closed forest and makes the pond part of its nightly foraging route. Swallows circle endlessly over the pond, plucking insects on the wing. Smaller birds forage along the edges or come down to the water to drink. Ducks may have taken up residence at the pond, if it is large enough, and can be seen with their young dabbling along the pond shallows. Their tracks sketch delicate patterns along the muddy banks and blend with those of the raccoon and weasel to form a beautiful tapestry. Closer looks reveal tiny tracks of insects and amphibians. In fact, the mud frame of the pond is covered by thousands of different tracks, each a page of an animal's life and habits, there for anyone who knows how to read them.

Wherever there is water, there is a wealth of animals that will use it. Because it supports a wide variety of plants that the animals can feed on, water will make any area come alive. And water, added to a forest, field, or brush tangle, will increase the wildlife-carrying capacity of the land.

Streams and drainage ditches can draw the same fauna and flora, though drainage ditches only run during certain times of the year or during heavy rains. (Streams, except in extreme drought, will run virtually year-round.) The drainage ditches will only be used by the animal population during the times water is running. The vegetation found along even dried drainage ditches is more succulent and varied than that of the surrounding areas and will still draw animals, though in lesser numbers. Some of these drainage systems will contain some water for several months, and the local wildlife, especially the reptiles and amphibians, will use these areas for their young, moving on when the areas finally dry up. By keeping track of these drainage ditches, you can plot the high times of the year, when the animals will use them the most, and plan your observation times accordingly.

A blind set by the edge of a pond, stream, or drainage ditch will produce grand results. It should be located back from the edge and nestled into the thicker vegetation. Dawn and dusk will be the best times to see the more secretive predators, but the ponds are active all day, even at high noon. A problem with waterways close to civilization is that they can be polluted by runoff that includes gas, oil, garbage and street waste. This pollution can affect the animals that inhabit the waterways. It is not uncommon after a rain to see fish killed by these pollutants floating atop a pond or stream. The pollutants will also affect the biosphere and render it virtually sterile. Ponds can become good indicators of the general health of the area. Just like we use blood tests to determine diseases, the earth's blood can be tested to find the overall health of the land.

ANIMAL LIFE

Bluegill sunfish (*Lepomis macrochirus*)

Every day, during the spring and summer months, my little boy would go down to our farm pond to feed his fish. He had no need for an aquarium because the countless sunfish and bass that lived in our pond provided endless enjoyment. He would spend hours collecting worms, small insects, and larvae, and take those, along with some bread, down to the pond's edge, just as the sun was warming the outer edges of the water. Stomping on the edge of the pond as a way of calling "his fish," he would soon have hundreds of sunfish awaiting his handout. He would spend hours feeding the fish, watching their habits with utter fascination, and becoming totally enraptured by the whole affair.

Some of the larger fish he knew by name, because of some unique marking or scars on their bodies. I was fascinated every time he took me to the pond's edge, because even with his untrained childlike observation skills, he would point out habits that would be missed by the most careful observer. He became so much a part of the pond system that he could actually swim with the fish and they would follow him, unafraid, just as a pet dog would follow its master. By midsummer, some of the larger sunfish would actually let him stroke their undersides and heads and seem to relish the human touch. At one time I watched him gently lift a large sunfish from the water, an act that suggested the total trust of the fish. There is a definite spiritual, emotional, and physical communication between all children and nature, which children can enjoy if parents give them the freedom to explore.

Sunfish are an intriguing fish. At first they look rather relaxed, basking readily in the sun. But don't let the looks fool you, for they are voracious and vicious feeders, and when defending their territory during mating season, they exhibit a vigor that would rival a bass. In fact, many times I've witnessed a sunfish drive off a bass many times larger than itself with repeated lungings and evasive swimming.

Sunfish range in color from yellowish-green to dark blue. There are about eight irregular verticle dark lines on the body, which help to camouflage the fish in the thicker weeds. At the end of the gill the adults have a black appendage, or flap, and another black blotch near the rear of the dorsal fin.

The pectoral fins are long and pointed, giving the sunfish a look of graceful elegance. The mouth may appear small but it will astonish you at what it can devour. Some of the larger sunfish can grow to fourteen inches long and four pounds. In the Northern climates the fish will grow at a rate of about one inch per year; in the more Southern locales they can grow up to four inches per year. The male creates a nest, which is a shallow, concave depression in the bottom of the pond. The females are enticed into these nests and will lay up to 35,000 eggs, which will hatch in about five days. The male voraciously protects the eggs and the young fry until they are old enough to leave the nest. The male tends to keep the nest immaculately clean.

Most sunfish prefer the quiet weedy waters in sunny shallows. The larger sunfish, however, will sometimes contradict this preference, sticking instead to the deeper waters, only visiting the shallows to feed in the morning and late afternoon. The primary food of the sunfish are insects, some aquatic plants, and even smaller crustaceans. In closed farm ponds the bluegill population may become limited both in size and number unless predator fish are kept in check and proper food is available. The little bluegill sunfish is one of the most fascinating pond dwellers and lends itself to study quite easily. They are quite easily trained to accept food and can be a source of enjoyment for children of all ages.

Water strider (*Gerris spp.*)

On our ponds is an insect that is both intriguing and a bit hypnotic. The ability of the water strider to walk across the surface of water with utter ease and speed is utterly astonishing. If you sit quietly for a while next to any pond, the water striders will emerge and put on a grand show as they dance across the surface in search of food. Sometimes you might even swear they are playing for your benefit rather than going about their daily chores. For me, no pond or stream is complete without the water strider, and there are species to capture anyone's fancy. There are even species that will exist in salt water. Some can remain submerged for quite some time, while others will die very quickly if left underwater for any length of time. The water strider winters under rocks or partially submerged sticks but on warmer days of winter can be seen scurrying about the surface of the water.

Upon close examination of the water strider you will find that each pair of legs have a different function. The first pair are for grasping, the second and third pair for diving and swimming, and the mid pair for resting on the surface tension of the water. Some water striders have wings and some do not. The variations are endless and are a good source of study. Just as you think you have learned everything about the water strider, it will take on a new habit that will rock you back to square one.

The body of the water strider is about one-half-inch long, and the legs are much longer. Even though the water strider prefers quiet waters, I have seen them on the jetties that buffer the waters of the ocean, apparently unaffected by the pounding surf. Their food consists of insects that are captured near the surface or just below. Sometimes I have witnessed the striders actually jump up and snag an insect in midair. Their feeding habits are a marvel, especially when they stalk up to unsuspecting prey as stealthily as a mountain lion, careful not to make even the slightest ripple to give away their presence. Their escape is usually by rapid erratic flight across the water that leaves a rather impressive wake. If frightened, they can hide so well as to be undetected.

People are always fascinated by the striders for their ability to walk easily on water. Even with a magnifying glass on them, you can hardly detect a dent they make on the surface. Their movements produce barely a ripple. Many freeze and become like small sticks when predators are about, but there are few animals that will take the time and effort to feed on this elusive insect. I have successfully kept them in an aquarium, but eventually they become a little skittish, fail to eat, and die. I now only keep the striders for a day or two to study their intricate habits and their ever-fascinating ability to walk on water.

Back swimmer (family Notonectidae)

One of my first encounters with a back swimmer was a rather painful one. I had spent many months as a child exploring the various ponds of our neighborhood and collecting all sorts of fauna and flora. The back swimmers always intrigued me, but they were more difficult to catch than the water striders and the whirligig beetles. With the aid of a fine-mesh collecting net I was fortunate enough to collect one of these elusive little insects. Upon transferring it into my collecting jar, it stung me, ejecting a whitish fluid. I was stung just above the hand near the wrist, and in no time my wrist swelled up and became very painful. I decided that the best place to observe the back swimmer was in its natural environment and my aquarium was no place for such a nasty creature. In the years that followed and in the countless ponds I have frequented, I have never been stung again, so I've chalked the whole affair up to a freak accident. I knew very well, however, that the back swimmer gives chase to its usually small prey and paralyzes them by stinging, so I've never taken the chance again of making one angry.

The back swimmer is about one-half-inch long and its body is shaped much like a boat. Most of its life is spent swimming on its back in search of prey. The back of the back swimmer is dark and the underside is a creamy, nearly beige, color. Upon close inspection you will find that the front legs are for grasping prey, the mid pair are for holding prey or clinging to bits of debris in the water, and the rear pair act as very effective oars, which can propel it through the water, even strong currents, rather quickly.

The eyes of the back swimmer are quite large and sport numerous hairs for underwater protection from predators. Along the submerged "underside" is a trough covered by hair, which I suspect helps it maintain buoyancy and gives it a supply of oxygen. The back swimmer has been known to fly at night and land belly-down. Sometimes, with a dull light you can catch the flight of the back swimmers. There are many species of back swimmers; usually it is the larger species that live on the surface and the smaller ones that live just beneath. Some of the smaller ones will actually feed on tiny crustaceans. If you are quiet, you can hear a faint whirring sound given off by certain species. When first heard, this sound is very exciting but rather eerie.

Back swimmers are fun to watch in their seemingly random movements. They seem to play more than most other animals, but that is most likely a matter of romantic interpretation. Nonetheless, they are wonderful to watch. As always, the more you study an animal the more you detect new habits and the more you realize what is left to be learned. Even something as seemingly uncomplicated as a back swimmer can take a lifetime to fully understand yet only a few quiet moments to enjoy. It is fun to know that just outside your backyard is a wealth of animal life just waiting to be explored and appreciated. Each sighting transports the observer out of the suburban environment and to another time and place where things are again pure and natural.

Painted turtle (*Chrysemys picta*)

This is by far one of my favorite pond turtles, not only because of its gorgeous coloration but also because of its ability to exist right near the haunts of man. The painted turtle is a fun turtle to study and it doesn't take much skill to observe them. They love the sun, especially on warm spring and summer days. When you first approach a pond, the turtles will slide off the half-submerged logs that they use as sunning spots into the safety of the water. After sitting quietly for a while, you will notice their tiny heads edge up from the water's surface as they look around to see if all danger has passed. Then slowly, sometimes laboriously, depending on how far the sunning log or rock sticks out of the water, they will make their way back up to their perch, where they will quickly fall asleep. In certain areas where sunning logs are scarce, you can find several turtles stacked one on top of the other like saucers. Rarely do they sun on the shore, due to heavy predation. Painted turtles cannot close themselves into their shells like the box turtle can.

The painted turtle is beautifully colored. Its upper shell is a polished dark olive and edged by random stripes, blotches, and patterns of various hues of red. Its underside is a rich yellow, the front being lobed and the rear being wide and unnotched. Painted turtles can grow to about seven inches long, though I have seen them larger. They are about 4½ inches wide on the top and 2-2½ inches thick. The lower part, or the plastron, can grow to 6 inches long and about 3½ inches wide. The female is larger than the male when full grown. They both hibernate during the colder winter months.

The painted turtle is a lover of ponds and usually-quiet waters, even in close proximity to man, if the food and cover is adequate. In areas of the Toms River in New Jersey, I have seen the painted turtles in the stronger currents, seemingly unaffected by the faster water. They will feed on aquatic plants and animals, dead or alive. The painted turtle is also a scavenger and cleans up much of the organic garbage of the ponds, thus keeping them fresh. Most of their food is eaten underwater, so it takes a mask and snorkel to witness their feeding habits. It is a real treat to watch the magical world unfold just a few inches below the surface. Very few people ever know the rapture and beauty of the underwater world of ponds.

Once when walking across the clear ice of a Pine Barrens lake, I noticed beneath the ice a number of painted turtles emerge from the mud and feed on the dead vegetation near the bottom. Even though the lake was iced over, the sun could penetrate into the shallower parts and warm the water enough to stir the turtles from their sleep. As soon as the sun passed and the sunspots "dried up," the turtles beat a hasty retreat back into the thick mud at the lake's bottom.

Dragonfly (*Libellcila spp.*)

What pond is complete without the erratic helicopter flight of the local dragonflies? Truly, they are real acrobats, able to hover, change direction in a heartbeat, and travel at tremendous speeds with barely a whisper from their wings. They are always a treat to watch as they search for food over the ponds. Watching closely, you may see them turn their heads from side to side, as they scan all parts of their domain for danger, food, or a place to rest. There are many species of dragonflies and their kin; each is unique in its own ways, coloration, and habits.

Dragonflies have four wings that are held horizontally at right angles to the body when they are resting. The wings in themselves are beautiful, usually opaque and lavished with an intricate netting of veins and patterns of colors. They are streamline in appearance, with long and slender abdomens and medium-size legs. Their heads are large and highly agile, with eyes that are large and bulging. Their mouth parts are for chewing and quite ominous-looking.

The dragonfly nymphs are aquatic and have even more impressive jaws. The lower jaws can be extended to a huge gaping orifice to help them gobble up larger prey. Their appetites are huge. There are thousands of dragonflies and their kin known to man—some suggest over 7,000 different types—so there is no danger of running out of dragonflies to study. The average flying height of a dragonfly is often a good indicator of the species. Darnets like to fly high above the ponds, while skimmers lower. Spotted dragonflies prefer to fly between five and six feet above the water, while the argias species fly just less than two feet above. This habit, I guess, has something to do with food preference and where above the pond surface the most preferred insects will be located.

The male dragonfly has a clasper at the end of its abdomen for reproduction purposes. It will hold the female by the neck while mating; sometimes the pair can be seen flying along piggyback for quite some time until impregnation is insured. The female will drop, or more often place, her eggs in the water, into various plant tissues or right into the mud. The nymph—the aquatic, undeveloped dragonfly—will feed mostly on larvae of various water insects. Some may feed on tadpoles, tiny fish or any other animal small enough to catch. Dragonflies can take up to two years to mature. The adults will feed on insects that they catch on the wing. With their erratic powerful flight, they can outmaneuver most pond-oriented insects and in turn help keep the population of harmful insects down.

The dragonflies are sun lovers and the more blessed the day is with rich sunshine, the more dragonflies will be seen. Though not communally-oriented they will roost in considerable numbers at night. My son and I, with the aid of a flashlight, scan the weedy sections of the ponds in search of these small dragonfly clusters. Even though their powerful mouths can deliver a good bite, they are much more docile at night, and some will even allow you to pet them between the wings if you are gentle and careful enough. I like to think that they enjoy this petting, and it tends to bring us closer in kinship with our dragonfly neighbors.

Pickerel frog (*Rana palustris*)

Who of us cannot visit the ponds and fail to notice the pickerel frogs that are so numerous along our banks and water edges? Every pond comes alive with a wide assortment of music, especially in the evening, when the deep bass voice of bullfrogs combine with those of the leopard frogs, the green frogs and the pickerel frogs. For me there is no greater music in the world and when sitting beside a small pond at night and listening to this symphony of animal life that surrounds me, I have a sense of what "stereo" really means. One of my favorite frogs is the pickerel frog, not simply because of its voice, coloration, or habits but also because it inhabits places that many of its relatives would never dream of living in. Even a slimy drainage ditch on the edge of town can become home for one of these beautiful little beasts. It is probably one of the first frogs we ever captured as children.

The easiest way to capture one of the pickerel frogs, or for that matter any frog, is at night with the use of a flashlight. For some reason the bright light causes them to freeze and your hand can easily be slipped in from behind and the frog grabbed. My son and I have spent many hours combing the ponds and collecting frogs. (You must explain, as I have to my son, that the frogs are delicate, though slippery, and should be grasped gently so as not to hurt them.) When I collect frogs, I keep them in my terrarium for a few days to listen to their music and study them, then I let them go back to where they belong. I hate capturing and keeping any animal for long periods of time, because their habits change to the new environment and I can tell instinctively that they are unhappy. Still the best way to study them is at close hand, and the music they provide at night will lull you to sleep like the sweetest of lullabies.

The pickerel frog is not very large as frogs go. The males are about 2¾ inches long and the females slightly smaller, though in warm ponds with good food I have seen them slightly bigger. The male is the croaker of the group and lets out a grand beckoning tone to females. The sound of hundreds of them calling together is something wonderful to hear. The males also sport a swollen thumb during breeding time, so that they can clasp onto the female while mating.

The pickerel frog markings are beautiful. It is not as dramatic as a green frog or a bullfrog but has, in its own right, splendid coloration that blends well for effective camouflage. The camouflaging doesn't work all the time, however, for on a few occasions my boy and I have watched a great blue heron gobble up quite a few; bass also relish them. The slight poison on its skin, which makes it taste a bit bitter, seems little deterrent to a hungry predator. Down their elegant green backs are two regular rows of squarish, black spots that have very definitive black borders. The hind legs are a pale yellow, which continues upward to mid-abdomen. In most areas the coloration blends beautifully with the muck and vegetation of the pond, making them almost invisible except to the careful observer, and occasional heron.

They are lovers of ponds but can also be found near streams and lakes in large numbers. During dry weather or when ponds are beginning to dry up, you may find them wandering overland in search of new water systems. They don't stay out in the open much during these journeys but prefer to stick close to the damper, more shaded areas. At one time I saw a small group of them traveling across a busy highway, seeking refuge at the other side where a small pond was located. Apparently the ditch they were living in had dried up and could no longer support their population. And once, I found a pickerel frog four miles from water; it had traveled for several days in search of a new water source and eventually found a new pond. For the life of me I could not tell how it knew where the pond was or whether it was just dumb luck.

The pickerel frogs breed and lay their eggs in shallow water. The eggs are bright yellow and in a globular gelatinous mass that is either free-floating or attached to a submerged object such as a rope or boat rigging. A female can lay up to 2,000 eggs, which will hatch in one to three weeks, depending on the conditions, and will, in about eighty days, become tadpoles of about three inches in length. The tadpoles sport a deep purple, almost opaque, tail with an iridescent blue at various other parts. They feed on the slime of decomposing plants and animals, while the adults feed primarily on insects but will also eat, on occasion, worms and any other small animal they can catch and kill. The tadpole usually takes a full year to turn into a frog but will not be ready to breed for two or three years, depending on conditions.

Barn swallow (*Hirundo rustica*)

One of my greatest thrills is to sit quietly at the edge of a pond in the late afternoon or when the sun is on its way down and watch the splendid aerial acrobatics of the swallows—diving, wheeling, swooping, and turning in the wink of an eye to catch some unsuspecting insect. At times they'll skim the surface of the water picking up insects or taking a drink on the wing. Once, however, I watched a huge bass leap from our pond and grab a young swallow that had slowed in its flight above a particularly quiet part of the pond. I find that the heat of the late day is the best time to watch the swallows in great numbers, since the air is warm and the insects are plentiful.

I often watch the swallows gathering near the muddy areas, collecting mud for their nests. Each mouthful is carried back to an old building, barn, or under the protective eaves of a house and is packed together into a beautiful, cup-shaped nest. The final touch is a lining of fine grasses or string, hair, or down from certain plants. The nests seem to be so precariously placed that the fact they hold fast seems to me a tremendous feat of engineering. The eggs of the barn swallow are white, or white with spots of brown or even purple, and usually hatch within two weeks. If you are lucky enough to have an old shed or barn where the swallows have built their nests, you can easily set up an impromptu blind that will conceal your presence but allow you to get remarkably close. Barn swallows have a great tolerance for man and as long as you do not touch the nest, move too quickly, or visit it too often, you can observe the young grow, fledge, and join the ranks of these aerial acrobats.

Another place barn swallows can be seen is on telephone wires. If the wires are close enough to the ground and near a feeding area, they will use them as roosts. It's odd how they all sit at exact distances apart, coming and going in small groups to feed. In late summer long strings of wire will be covered with swallows, a last gathering before the long trip south. When they are sitting so close, you can also see the differences between the males and females quite clearly. The male has a chestnut-brown forehead, but in some areas of the country it can be a deep steel blue. They have a dark chestnut brown on the chin and throat, which slowly drifts back to lighter coloration. The female is smaller than the male and a little duller in color. You will note also that their tails are more deeply forked than other swallows'. To me their legs and feet look far too small for their bodies, as if they belonged to another bird. I think that is why they are rarely seen sitting on the ground. They are also a little awkward when taking flight from the ground, which may be because of their small legs.

The food of the barn swallow consists of all kinds of animals, caught usually on the wing, especially near ponds and bodies of water. They prefer mosquitoes, flies, bees, wasps, and almost anything that flies about the water areas. For some reason they will stay away from certain kinds of insects, such as honey bees and a few others, but will eat other stinging insects without any ill effects. I just can't understand why they'll eat some and not others. Barn swallows nesting near your home will make your life much easier, since they will cut down on many of the insect pests that plague us. I am an advocate of leaving up old sheds and other buildings simply because they provide suitable nesting sites and encourage the swallows to stay close to our homes.

Great blue heron (*Ardea herodias*)

The great blue heron was an important bird to Rick and I as children. It, along with the mountain lion, was the chief teacher of stalking. The mountain lion taught us how to use our feet—to touch, roll and add pressure, but the great blue heron taught us how to hold our upper body. Your feet could be absolutely quiet as you stalked your quarry, but if your upper body attitude was not perfect, all the stealth of the foot was for naught. You would still scare the game. We would sit quietly in the brush at the side of a pond or waterway and watch the heron stalk for fish. Or we would watch it walk the lower marshy fields and hunt for mice, snakes, frogs, and other animals.

Grandfather considered the heron one of the master teachers, a true grandfather of the stalk and the hunt, lightning fast in its accuracy, perfect in its stillness. It was in this ability to become absolutely still, to adopt a gentle, almost imperceptible flow of motion, that made the heron a master fisherman. The heron taught us how to read water and thrust our spears with accuracy. It taught us also how to walk the muddy pond bottoms without stirring up clouds of mud or losing our footing. We would practice for hours the heron walk, holding our bodies absolutely still, moving only our eyes, and allowing our legs to flow forward, slowly and imperceptibly. To improve our balance we would stand on one leg as the heron did at rest, or balance and stalk in a very muddy area of a swamp. The heron's motion, whether on water or on land, became our mode of stalking. Many cultures learn their stalking or hunting methods from the herons. Even many of the martial arts use certain heron ways for poise, balance, and fighting.

The great blue heron is an intriguing bird, whether standing stoically at the edge of a pond like some old weathered stump or flying so slowly and elegantly across the skies. I have seen the heron in many parts of the country, in watery areas right next to busy highways, housing projects, factories, and even in the petroleum-cracking areas of northeastern New Jersey where the waterways wash right along major pipelines and highways. Even New York City's Central Park sports a dramatic population of great blue herons. It is very ironic that a bird so big can live within a stone's throw of the most densely populated areas without ever being noticed. But that shouldn't shock me, for I wonder how many commuters really *see* the sun rise or set through their windshields, or the hawks circling over the roadways, or the peregrine falcons hunting pigeons outside their office windows.

The great blue heron is about forty-five to fifty inches in length, with a long sharp bill of up to six inches, possibly more. Their legs and necks are elegantly long and slender. In spite of their size and grace, these birds are, amazingly enough, overlooked much of the time. They are pale bluish gray with a patch of white at the center of their throat. Near the shoulder of the wing is a gorgeous swatch of chestnut. The breast is lightly streaked with black and white, and their legs are black. The young birds have a blackish crown.

The heron feeds primarily on fish, consuming some up to a foot, or more, long. They catch the fish by silently stalking the water's edge, about knee-deep, pausing at times to watch for the movement of fish. The fish seem to pay them little attention, probably because from underwater they appear much like a log or pole, or even a cluster of brushy sedge. Once a fish is spotted, the heron slowly moves its head into position, sometimes holding that pose for a long time. Finally, in a lightning flash, it will plunge its head into the water and spear the fish. It hunts the same way for snakes, grasshoppers, mice, frogs, crayfish, or any other animal it can catch.

If you are lucky enough to live near a heron breeding area, you can easily spot the nests, because they are a loose platform of sticks precariously balanced in trees. These nests can be used year after year, and once one is located, you will have many fine seasons of watching the mating, fledgling, and rearing processes of these birds. Usually they lay three or four pale blue eggs, which take about twenty-eight to thirty days to hatch. The young are scrawny, helpless, and fed regurgitated animal matter from the parents. In the northern breeding areas, the young are ready to fly by mid July.

If you are interested in teaching your children the art of stalking or in learning yourself from one of the experts, then the herons are the ones to watch. I know many trout fishermen that have studied the herons in order to improve their methods of wading streams and ponds, without stirring up the bottom and scare the fish.

A cousin to the great blue heron is the cattle egret, which is expanding its range and can be found in many parts of this country. Like the heron, the egret is an excellent stalker. These white birds, about half the size of the great blue, will follow livestock around the fields and eat those animals they scare from the brush. It is not uncommon to see a cattle egret perched on the back of a steer or walking between its front feet, seemingly just out of danger of being stepped on. These egrets are also grand teachers of stalking and of movement in general.

Brown bullhead catfish (*Ictalurus nebulosus*)

The catfish is usually one of the first fish caught by youngsters. I have many fine memories of leisurely fishing for catfish on quiet ponds on lazy late summer days. I respect the catfish for its ability to exist under conditions and in areas where other fish would surely perish. It is a mysterious fish of the muck and dark waters and has astounding powers of locating prey. Grandfather, Rick, and I would go to the slow upper reaches of the muddy Toms River tributaries, especially near the eddies at night. There, with the use of torches made from tallow-soaked cattails, we would fish for the catfish, using any kind of bait we could find in our local garbage cans. The lights from our torches would attract them by the hundreds, and we would end up feeding them by hand instead of fishing, though we always caught a few, because the meat was one of our favorites. The catfish was one of the first fish I effectively speared during a survival situation, since it was an easy mark for my primitive fishing bow.

Catfish are mysterious also because of the way they seem to come from nowhere. They'll thrive in ponds that seem too small to support any fish at all. I have seen catfish live for long periods in ponds that were all but dried up and the fish were only barely covered by thick muddy water. Later, when the pond refilled with runoff, the catfish had survived. For reasons I still do not know, I have even seen them out of the water on the banks. For me, they seem the essence of the ancient fish, the proverbial monster of the blackened depths. Every time I catch a big one and look at its huge mouth and ominous spines, I shudder at the memory of larger catfish pulling under baby ducks and even swallowing small turtles whole.

Catfish usually grow to about twenty inches long, but much larger ones have been caught, especially down South in the warmer muddy waters. I've heard that the record catfish was near 150 pounds. Their coloration is a remarkable blend for camouflage in their preferred environment. They range from a deep olive to dark brown, with dark mottlings, usually on the sides, that fade to a white, beige, or yellow underbelly. They have no scales and their skin is slimy, making them hard to hold. Sharp spines on the pectoral and dorsal fins can inflict nasty wounds, however, to the inexperienced handler. They have sensitive sensing organs that can detect potential prey at long distances, and they have a grouping of taste organs on the undersides.

The male usually makes a nest in the mud. Mating takes place in the spring, and the female will lay up to 2,000 eggs, which will hatch within five days. The male protects the young coal-black fish well into the summer. Swarms of these little fish can be seen in the shallows with the protecting male most often close by. The catfish loves quiet, warm, and muddy waters, but I have seen them in fresher waters and even in streams with strong currents, though they were found in the eddies along the banks. The catfish feeds on insect larvae, crustaceans, fish, or just about anything it can catch. A big thrill is to swim in muddy waters with a face mask and skirt the muddy banks of the ponds or slow rivers to find numerous catfish—an awesome and scary sight, especially if you spot some of the larger ones.

PART II:
URBAN WILDERNESS

Though the urban wilderness is covered by buildings, houses, sidewalks, streets and parking lots, there is still a wide variety of wildlife that can be seen—if the city dweller knows how and where to look. That this wilderness goes so often undiscovered is not because people are incapable of observation, but because they simply do not know what kinds of wildlife there are to be found. If you don't even suspect the presence of a wild animal, why would you spend precious time and energy looking for one? But the city *is* a jungle, one different than our usual conceptions of wilderness, but a wilderness nonetheless. To many animals the city is little different from a cliff dwelling, and a building or a street is much like a sparse mountain slope.

Generally, the city environment can be divided into different ecological environments. Each environment—streets, alleys, sewers, abandoned lots, waterfronts, playgrounds, and parks—will house and feed its own diverse population of animals and plants, but it is important to keep in mind that animals are free roamers and may move from one area to another. Despite the severe, often sterile conditions, these animals have adapted well to these landscapes and to the close, almost incessant, proximity of people, buildings, and vehicles. These animals tend to be stealthier than their country and wilderness cousins, making them more difficult to spot and track, but they are there for anyone who ventures out to look.

STREETS

The city streets and parking lots are rough country for wildlife, yet it is there (though not admittedly in the abundance you would find in suburban locations). These areas are frequented during the day by pigeons, sparrows, and finches, and other animals I'll discuss later. They congregate around the eateries of man, foraging for scraps of food that have fallen from garbage cans or inadvertently been dropped. They can be found in the most barren locations, but there must be *some* source of food to draw them. They roost and nest in the buildings, in the eaves, atop ledges or underneath. To them the city buildings are much like giant rock outcroppings, affording good cover from enemies and the weather; in a storm you can find the great populations of birds huddled to the lee side of buildings. Drinking water is obtained from puddles after a rain or from places that are always damp. During drought conditions I've seen pigeons fly several blocks in search of the nearest water source.

At night, when the traffic on the city streets and sidewalks is at its lowest, many of the more secretive animals begin to wander. Their homes are the back alleys, abandoned buildings and tiny crevasses all along this rock jungle. These animals have truly become masters of deception, camouflage, and stalking, able to move about with great ease yet escape detection. I once watched a weasel on the Lower East Side of Manhattan emerge from a small opening between buildings and thread its way to a parking lot to hunt mice at a local garbage pile. It clung to the curbs, moving only when it was sure there was no danger. When a person or car passed, it remained frozen, even in the exposed areas, and appeared as if it were nothing more than a lump of garbage.

The city streets and parking lots are certainly foraging grounds for some animals, but they are more important as highways of travel to the various feeding grounds. These areas are not usually a good place to watch the animals, because of the secretive way they use them, but you might have fairly good luck around waste baskets and other trash areas. It would not be uncommon to see weasels, raccoons, opossums, mice, rats, or other small rodents traveling the roads, slinking in and out of cover as they head for their established rounds of feeding. At night during the summer you can sometimes find bats in search of the insects that have been drawn to the lights.

Once after a speaking engagement in New York City that finished quite late, I walked the twenty-six blocks back to my car, my route taking me late at night through a deserted business district. I quietly made my way through the piles of trash that awaited for the morning garbage pickup. A stirring came from one of the trash piles, so I backed to the side of a building to watch. The noise was too loud and broad to be a rat and too clumsy to be a cat; I waited, not knowing what to expect. To my amazement a mother raccoon exited the trash pile followed by three young ones. One of the small coons let out a characteristic churring sound, and the mother turned around and clubbed it. They disappeared down a small opening between two buildings, an opening too small for me to go through. Such was the lesson given in the quietude of the city streets.

In Chicago, after another speaking engagement, I encountered an even more surprising city dweller when I walked late at night to my hotel. Passing by a small overgrown area, I caught sight of a movement out of the corner of my eye. I thought at first that it might be a hunting weasel, so I slowly stalked toward the bushes. I peered inside the bush, and, in the illumination of the street light, saw resting on a lower limb a rat snake swallowing a small mouse. Slowly it slipped off into the rubble, then down a crack in the railroad ties that bordered the garden. Upon closer inspection of the garden the next day, the tracks and scat revealed to me that the snake had hunted this area for quite some time. I do not know how a snake like that got into this small garden—probably someone's escaped pet—but the tracks indicated that it was doing rather well.

Repeatedly I have been amazed by the wildlife of the city streets. One night spent carefully watching a side street, especially one with a good collection of trash, will reveal some startling finds. One night on the outskirts of Philadelphia, I sat behind a small pile of restaurant garbage at the edge of a parking lot. In the span of four hours I saw three raccoons, one opossum, two weasels, countless mice and rats, bats, insects, and even a toad that had taken up residence under a pile of boards. Since the area was close to an open runoff sewer that held water most of the time, and to an unending pile of garbage, the area was a tremendous draw for animals—all streetwise, all secretive, and all with their well-protected homes. The area was located only a few feet off a city street but was infrequently used by cars or pedestrians during the evening and night hours, when the animals were most active.

I always look at the city streets as the highways of the city animal populations. So effectively secretive is their use of the streets that no one takes notice, not even of the braver feral cats and dogs. Though an area may serve the animals only for transit and not living or feeding, a close observer can be rewarded with myriad animal sightings. If one learns to look to the shadows, the hidden places, the edges of buildings, and the secret areas of our roadways and sidewalks, the rewards of animal sightings will be absolutely incredible.

To determine which animals are frequenting the roadways and sidewalks during the day or night, check for tracks and other signs around dirt areas—small squares of exposed earth around trees, or the sandy base of a parking meter, or even the silt that has collected in the gutters between the sidewalks and streets. I even look to the spilled milk shakes, ketchup, or other thick pasty delights for evidence of footprints. Many times I have found prints in the oil spots of parking areas and even in small gardens and windowboxes. A little careful observation of these areas will reveal the incredible variety of animals that use our city streets right along with us.

ABANDONED LOTS AND ALLEYS

The city streets, the highways of the urban animal world, connect various living areas and give a wide range and mobility to the animals. Though these streets are traveled, some more frequently than others, they are not the best areas for the citybound naturalist to observe animal movements. The abandoned lots and alleys are the areas the animals will frequent the most, for here is their food supply and their homes. These alleys and lots are the centers for the citybound animal's existence, with each lot and alley housing any number and variety of animals, depending on conditions. With a little knowledge of what produces the most animals in any given area, the naturalist can pick the areas that will be the most fruitful for animal observation and let the others go.

Generally, the more littered and isolated the lot or alley, the more animals it will contain. Abandoned lots in the older parts of the city will have more animals than those of the newer parts. Lots and alleys around abandoned buildings will have more animals than those next to occupied dwellings. Those located near bodies of water, piles of garbage, or with easy access to other abandoned lots and alleys, will have even more animals and greater varieties. I always seek out the bare-ground lots that have random piles of rubbish. The more silt and dust that collects in the lot, the more chance that plants will grow. Plants of any sort are a good indicator that the lot or alley provides a good place for animals.

Animals need a good source of food, good cover to escape enemies, and water. If you find these three elements, you have an excellent opportunity to observe some of the urban animals that go unnoticed by so many millions of people every day. To find a good observation location, you must choose with care, using the various signs and tracks of animals as indicators of what is where. Not knowing what to expect leaves you at a disadvantage when setting up your blind or camouflaging. The more you know about an animal, the more you will see it, as I tell my students time and time again. Remember that the city animal is just different enough from its country cousin to pose distinct tracking problems for you. That is why a good observer in the wilderness may not be so good in a city or suburban environment.

I try to encourage those of my students who live in the city to create animal areas within their neighborhoods. I ask them to find an abandoned lot and make conditions there ideal for animals to find shelter and food. Plant some hearty wild vegetation in the area, stack debris in an irregular fashion to create artificial caves, and add to the area what you would feel would bring in animals. Try to interest and involve the neighbors. If enough people get together, you might be able to obtain the owner's permission and create a natural, overgrown, gardenlike biosphere, which will attract more animals to the neighborhood. If more people turned abandoned lots into havens and gardens for animals, the tenor of a neighborhood just might change and the people become more in tune with the earth.

Many areas of our cities contain abandoned lots and abandoned buildings. Just think how much we could reclaim of the wonder of nature if we encouraged wildlife to these areas. Even the abandoned buildings could be made into homes for birds by putting up nesting boxes, supplying the proper building materials, and creating the environment they need. Turning our abandoned lots and alleys into little pockets of wilderness could bring mankind closer to a harmony with the natural world, and what a better place to start than in the barren and sterile jungles of our cities. Nature abhors a void and will fill it whenever possible. Just as a blade of grass will grow from a crack in a sidewalk, so will nature fill and reclaim any unused land. Any helping hand we can lend will make the process go so much faster, beautifying what was once considered ugly and abandoned.

I was once in Atlantic City for nearly five days, doing firsthand research on city and suburban survival, looking especially into the problems of the city at night. My days were free but the beaches were too tame and awash with people to do much close observation. At that time, large-scale casino construction was under way, and many casinos were already open. On the morning of my first day in the city, after a brief walk on the beach, I cut inland a little north of the city proper and began to walk back to my hotel. The area I walked through was under demolition but long periods had elapsed between the various stages, leaving a sea of abandoned lots and half-demolished buildings. It looked very much like a city that had been under siege and bombed out.

For some reason I was drawn to a lot that had been partially grown over by poison ivy and a smattering of seaside goldenrod. Feeding about the lot was a large assortment of small birds, mainly house sparrows, purple finches, and the ever-present pigeons. As I entered the area, I was brought abruptly to a halt by the sight of a fox track firmly planted in the sand. Easing my way through the area, I followed the fox tracks, which increased in frequency and led me from one abandoned lot to another, until I finally arrived at a rather large lot of mostly grasses. There, drifting in the final wisps of dawn mist, a fox slipped across the grass sea and disappeared into a cluster of cinder blocks in the center of the lot. I decided to come back later to investigate, when I was sure the fox was firmly bedded down for the day.

When the sun was at high noon, I cautiously stalked toward the cinder blocks. I knew how crafty a fox was under normal circumstances, and I suspected it would be even more so in a city. As I got to within a few yards of the blocks, some movement caught my eye, and to my delight, two young foxes were playing just outside a hole under the cinder blocks. The mother fox lay half asleep in the sun, never noticing me. I often look back on this experience and wonder why the mother fox never picked up my presence. In the wild, a mother fox would have easily spotted me. I wondered if the foxes were less wary in the city because people rarely notice them and thus pose little threat.

A few days later I found and approached another den a little north of where I found the first den. I had hardly entered the lot when I caught the dash of a fox into a hole near a partially demolished structure. I was puzzled a bit by this fox's opposite behavior to the fox I had seen the day before. I just couldn't figure out why one would run and one would take no notice at all. Was it the location that made the difference in the foxes' awareness? My questions were answered when I found a number of feral dog tracks in the area, intermingled with the tracks of a few tramps who lived in nearby abandoned buildings. Going back to the lot where I had seen the first fox, I found its tracks indicated that its cautiousness increased in certain areas, usually those that were open or contained some scent of danger. Thus, like the wilder fox, the city fox knew when to be cautious and when to lie back and take it easy.

The week I spent in that city was a real eye-opener in the sightings of animals I had never expected to find. One would assume that a city on a peninsula bordered by the Atlantic Ocean on one side and a bay at the other to have a fair amount of wildlife, but besides the smattering of ever-present shore birds, there was a wide assortment of animals that one wouldn't expect to find in an urban area: all sorts of mice, muskrat, rats, feral cats and dogs, voles, weasels, foxes, rabbits, skunks, raccoons, opossums, and bats. There were little islands of life filled with the scurry of feet, the songs of birds, and the scents of wildflowers everywhere.

In any city, small or large, one will always find that the alleys and the abandoned lots are filled with tremendous varieties of life, from the smallest insect to the larger mammals, from the thinnest sprout of grass to huge trees. All we have to do is look at the alleys and lots in a different way. View them as wildernesses rising out of waste lands—sterile at first glance but upon closer, educated investigation, vast resources teaming with interesting life, as nature fills every void with beauty.

PLAYGROUNDS AND PARKS

A playground or a park does not necessarily contain more animal life than the alleyways and abandoned lots of the city. Certainly, if the playground is used frequently, constructed on blacktop, and surrounded by dwellings, there will not be many animals. City parks may or may not have more animals than the abandoned lots, depending on how sterile and manicured the parks are. Parks with trimmed gardens and lawns and well-manicured trees, especially those parks that are heavily used, will not contain much wildlife, except for the token squirrels, pigeons, and sparrows. So, if you intend to do any serious animal watching in a park, you have to select one with care. Selecting the forgotten park that is less than manicured and sterile, or the playground that is bordered by infrequently cut weeds or hedgerows, will produce more wildlife than those of the formal variety.

Parks and playgrounds *can*, like the abandoned lots, be home to many fascinating animals and plants, if some land has been left unattended and overgrown. The rule of thumb for park or playground animal communities is the larger the park, the more animals will inhabit them. This circumstance is not only due to the amount of land but also due to the fact that the larger parks usually have more land that is not manicured and more that is not used frequently.

In New York City, Central Park is so large that it is impossible for the park crews to manicure the entire area. And even though the park is, on the whole, frequently used, a lot of land is left unattended and is an ideal habitat for a large variety of animals.

Many times after visiting the Museum of Natural History, I have spent time in Central Park, which is located directly across the street. In any season, at any time of the day or night, the park is alive with the goings and comings of myriad animals. In this park there are so many out-of-the-way places, thickets, rock outcroppings, and brush tangles that many animals feel right at home, though they have adopted city-learned traits. In variety of wildlife Central Park in New York City is no different from any other large urban park—whether in Chicago, Los Angeles, San Francisco, Dallas, or any other medium to large city. The smaller cities are usually surrounded by more parks and wilderness areas than the bigger urban sprawls and will contain more animal life.

One encounter in Central Park that turned me on to the wildlife that lives right under our urban noses came during one of my trips to the museum. I decided to eat lunch in the park on a set of rocks that were directly across from the museum. I drifted down from a trail and secluded myself in the bushes, leaning against a round rock that made a grand backrest. Blotting out the looming buildings and the sounds of the city, I drifted back in time to think of what the area must have looked like to the native peoples of America, when the land was still unspoiled. I imagined what it would have felt like for them to be camped near the rocks I sat upon, and I imagined the flow of wild animals from deer and bear, to cougar and wolf.

My daydreaming ended when my eyes came to rest on a discarded milk carton, which shocked me back into the reality of traffic noise and surrounding buildings, and I was saddened to think of what was lost. Then I caught sight of movement in front of the milk carton. There was something small and quiet, definitely a mouse of some sort. I stalked closer and was delighted to find not a house mouse but a white-footed mouse. The sight of the white-footed mouse brought me hope that there was a mystical unseen world of nature within the park, a world clinging easily to existence yet just out of reach of common, rushed man.

I stalked closer to the carton as the mouse went on its foraging run, and I took great care not to be seen or leave any traces of my scent that might scare the mouse away from its home. I lay on my belly and peered inside the milk carton, and there in a nest of shredded newspaper, grass, and pieces of woolen garment lay four pink baby white-footed mice—another generation of wilderness creatures, right in the center of one of the biggest cities in the world. For me, they created a doorway to the past, a link to thousands of past generations that had used this area when it was wild and free. To the mice, it was still a wilderness, wild and free.

I never made it back to the museum that day. Instead I spent most of the day and part of the night exploring the park's rock outcroppings and brush tangles. Raccoons slipped out of rock crevices, weasels drifted through the shadows like mirages, cottontails fed in grassy patches, birds clustered and sang from the brush tangles, and again I was transported to the days gone by. I lost all sense of time, the outside world disappeared, and I felt like I was one of the native spirits that still, according to Grandfather, lived in this place. Only after dark· was I yanked back to reality when a police officer spotted me atop a lookout rock and decided that my actions were a little strange. I was questioned and asked to leave, but I persuaded him to sit with me. Eventually he watched with childlike delight as a raccoon fed on the scraps from a garbage can just a few feet away.

In almost every city I have visited during my wandering days and book and speaking tours, I have repeated the Central Park scenario—always being delighted, intrigued, and awed by the wealth of animal life that clings to existence in the centers of the largest cities of the world. It brings me hope that wildlife persists, even in the most sterile environments, that mankind can still live in a balanced harmony with the natural world. I often wonder, while watching people play in the parks, how much they miss of the flow of natural life going on about them. If people could only abandon the rush of the city, slow down, and observe, they could be taken back to a different time and place and come closer to the natural world.

WATERFRONTS

In wilderness, country, or suburban and urban areas, water is like a magnet, a central draw, for wildlife, because all things need water. Whether at a small pond located high in the mountains of Yosemite, or the docks of the East River of New York City, or the Bay Area of San Francisco, waterfronts are magical places, abounding with wildlife, and in the cities, with animals and plants that can be found in no other urban area. Waterfronts can be by rivers, lakes, man-made ponds, drainage areas, low spots in city parks, and even the drainage ditches bordering our city streets. Wherever there is water, there is bound to be wildlife using it, although the more polluted the waters, the less wildlife will be found in an area.

Along the docks of New York City, especially those that are abandoned or less frequently used, generally people will see the feral cats and dogs, and the assortment of rats and mice, but far more animals are there than meet the untrained eye. Upon closer look, what you may think is a cat foraging the dock may actually be a raccoon, or what you may assume to be a rat could very well be a weasel. The food chain made possible by the waters makes life easier for the urban animals. Especially around larger bodies of water, such as lakes, rivers, and natural ponds, there is an abundant food chain, from the smallest particle of life to the larger animals.

Water is also a draw to the human animal. There is something magical about water, for it soothes the spirit and quiets the body. For us, water is at once a natural tranquilizer and also an exciting place to find wildlife. It becomes the best of both worlds, especially in a city, where the body needs solitude and calm. Before and after times of intense physical, mental, and emotional drain, whether in the country or during a speaking engagement in a city, I will instinctively seek out the water areas to help me think more clearly, relax, and introspect. Water is a great tranquilizer, providing a rush of emotion and excitement, especially for the city-bound naturalist and someone looking for escape for a few moments.

Once, before an important speaking engagement in Dallas, I sat by a fountain for a few hours contemplating what I was going to say and losing myself in the splash and rush of the water. In spite of the fact that the fountain was made of concrete and steel and had no vegetation around it, many local birds came to visit it.

Some drank, some bathed, and some foraged the insects that hid in the crevices of the surrounding rockwork. As the night came and it grew close to the time I had to deliver my speech, the stores around the fountain closed and the area became deserted. To my delight a raccoon came along, lumbered up the side of the fountain and took a long drink, and never noticed me sitting there. I observed this same raccoon arrive at the fountain for three straight nights with such precise timing that I could set my watch by it. In fact, its route up the side of the rock pool showed so much wear that it suggested its use went back several generations of raccoons.

When you look for wildlife at the water areas, especially at the larger lakes, ponds, and rivers, one of the first things you will notice is the variety and number of birds. Simply learning the various birds there, from gulls to sparrows, can keep a naturalist busy for days. Though surrounded by the cities, these animals exhibit many of the traits of their wilder relatives. Though they have adopted ways to live within the walls of civilization, their instincts for survival remain unchanged, and this fact affords a tremendous learning opportunity for the city-bound naturalist.

When I visit a city, I seek out the water areas, not only for a spiritual lift but also to see the huge variety of animals and plants that cluster there. From the water areas you can follow the animals to their various haunts in the city. The water areas are a center of animal activity and provide good starting points for studying animals in the urban environment.

ANIMAL LIFE

Gray squirrel (*Sciurus carolinensis*)

In any part of our cities with even a small grouping of trees, we are likely to see the gray squirrel, and we are likely to see them in larger numbers in the park areas. They have adapted well to the city environment and man and can become quite tame; some will even take food right from your hand. They are quite intelligent, having learned to approach people who frequently feed them and to be more wary of handouts from strangers. Their feeding habits in general are quite different from wilder squirrels, as they have learned to forage garbage areas and nearby eating establishments for all manner of food. Bits of bread, nuts, cereals, vegetables, seeds from rotten fruit, and the seeds of local weeds have become part of their diet. Watching the local squirrel population, or one individual for some time, you will discover established routes and feeding patterns. One gray squirrel in Chicago visited a local eating establishment only on the two days of the week when it knew garbage would be outside. Some squirrels will raid salad garbage only to pick out the sesame seeds and croutons.

Squirrels have been known to migrate because of food scarcity or overpopulation. I once witnessed one of these migrations during the late winter in New York's Central Park, when small groups of squirrels began moving north through their well-established aerial roadways. Some I followed for miles.

Trees, as well as providing homes for the city squirrel, afford protection from enemies. Their homes are usually built in tree hollows or in the typical leafy nests, but some city squirrels will even take over drainage pipes and hollows in building eaves, providing they are close enough to trees. Urban squirrels relish the tree nuts and buds and will store them in small quantities wherever they can find a good hiding spot, such as in a small garden, windowbox, or protected alcove. With their remarkable sense of smell, they locate these caches in the winter, though many of their stores are raided by rats, mice and other animals.

If you find a special little grove of city trees to frequent, it is easy to befriend the local squirrels and learn much from them. They do bite, however, so you should use caution when feeding them. They also get a little skittish and will not approach you if there are dogs, cats, or many people around, but don't give up—it takes time for any animal to gain confidence in you. Feed them nuts and grains rather than bread and pastries, which contain too much sugar and do the squirrel more harm than good. When feeding any city animal, it is best to give them the kind of food that is as close to their natural food as possible.

To bring squirrels to you, you should begin by sitting quietly where you have seen squirrels before. Toss about bits of food and wait patiently until they come around and begin to feed. They may not come near you for several days, but eventually they will accept you as no threat and begin to feed all around you. Once you have gained their confidence, hold out bits of food to them and toss some closer to where you're sitting. Within a week or so they will be sitting on your lap and taking food right from your hands—a thrill for any adult or child.

Gray squirrels grow to about eighteen inches long, including their beautiful plumelike tails, which they use for balance. Despite their plump appearance, they usually weigh only about a pound, but a well-fed city squirrel can be much heavier. Their coloration is absolutely beautiful, especially when viewed up close. Their underfur is slate colored, and the outer fur is speckled with black and white. If you observe a single hair closely, you will find it white-tipped over black, gray, or buff, depending on what part of the body it came from.

The gray squirrel mates in spring and two to six young are born, depending on the availability of food. The young will stay with the mother for a season, and at times you can see them playing together in the upper branches or around trunks. The young emerge from the nest about six weeks after birth but do not grow their full fur until they are eight to ten weeks old. Young squirrels have gorgeous eyes, which are large in proportion to their bodies. They look a little unsure, and thus produce an endearing image that is easily captured by even the amateur photographer.

When Rick and I were young, Grandfather had us study the squirrel in the same manner he had had us study other animals: imagining ourselves to be them, to see how they lived and interacted with the earth. The squirrel taught us much about climbing and moving about trees with ease. Though we could not climb like the squirrels, they did teach us enough about aboreal maneuvers to help us negotiate climbing, moving from one tree to another, and sitting for long periods of time aloft watching the ground-dwelling animals. Most important, the squirrel taught us one of the grandest lessons of survival: in studying their large leafy nests, we learned the secret that dead-air space played in insulation. We later incorporated this technique into making our shelters, thus creating huge squirrel-like nests on the ground. Still, today, after many thousands of hours of survival situations in all climates and weather, I have found that for shelter the modified squirrel nest is unsurpassed in warmth and comfort.

Little brown bat (*Myotis lucifugus*)

Who would ever think that in the city, of all places, one would see a bat? No, bats do not dwell in huge numbers in the city, because of the limited supply of insects, but nonetheless they are there. In New York, Chicago, Los Angeles, and Houston, I have seen them diving and wheeling around streetlights, city parks, pond areas, and waterfronts, as if they were totally oblivious to the horns, lights, people, traffic, and hustle going on below their aerial domain. Most of the people who see the common little brown bat in the city will mistake it for a large moth circling about the streetlights that draw all manner of insects during the night. A sure way to tell a bat from a larger moth or other insect is by its quick, erratic flight, which displays the ultimate in aerial acrobatics. And, if you can hear above the city drone, you might detect the high-pitched squeaks they use in locating their food.

Little brown bats will inhabit most areas of the city: city parks, waterfronts, abandoned lots, any place that insects make a home. Bats have a tremendous homing instinct and are able to fly more than thirty miles to find a good feeding location and still return by morning to their favorite roosting area. They will roost in houses, old trees, hollows of buildings, under eaves—in fact, in any place they can get out of the weather and the strong light. If there is any sort of an insect population around, there is sure to be a bat nearby. Once, when I was in a hotel, I looked down out of my window to a penthouse garden that was beautifully landscaped and saw not only a good assortment of insects buzzing about the lights but also a few bats. The people attending the rooftop party paid absolutely no attention to either the bats or the insects.

The little brown bat is about 3¾ inches long, with a tail that's a little over an inch. Its face is quite hairy, with narrow ears, and dark beady little eyes. The hair is long, soft, very luxurious, and dullish brown over lighter brown. Both sexes are colored alike and are about the same size. Even though the bats mate in the fall, the sperm does not fertilize the egg until the following spring. The female and male separate soon after the birth of the single offspring, the male stays away until the end of the brooding season. The young nurse for about twenty-four days, then are able to fly and forage on their own. Males and females will then begin mixing again. It is not uncommon to find several species of bats roosting together.

As a child I was once taken to the docks of New York Harbor to tour a naval ship that had been open to the public. My dad, having been a chief engineer during World War II, got to talking to some of the sailors and left my brother and I to explore the ship until well after dark. A warm breeze was blowing from the direction of New Jersey and carried with it a huge swarm of insects. At dusk, the swallows fed feverishly on the insects, and as soon as the sun set and the lights came on, so did the bats, literally by the thousands. For hours I watched them, forever on the wing, dashing, darting, changing direction in erratic patterns, and never tiring. The whole affair looked like some surrealistic celestial event, as groups of bats faded in and out of the lights, flashing now and then as the light reflected from their undersides. Then as if by magic, the night chilled, the breezes died, and the bats disappeared, along with most of the insects.

House mouse (*Mus musculus*)

The common house mouse is certainly a carrier of disease and destroys clothing, books, and stores of food, and even chews on the wood of our houses and apartments, but it is worth study. It is a wild animal, even though it likes to take up residence right alongside man. Some of the little critters even become so brazen that they literally have to be chased out of our cupboards with a stick. They are pests known to everyone, but very few people know much about their life history or unique habits. I think it's fascinating that an animal can live so close to us, even right under our noses and remain virtually unobserved. I admire animals that are smart enough to elude danger and not only survive but also flourish. Mice, like it or not, are part of our urban ecosystem.

Mice grow to about seven inches long, including a 3½-inch tail, though a well-fed mouse can be a little bigger. Both sexes sport a uniform brownish-gray fur, with slightly lighter underparts, and short, fine hair. Their noses and heads are pointed; their ears are large, rounded, and erect; and their bodies are slender and streamlined. They are able to get in and out of areas you would not think an animal of its size could, but they flatten themselves, contort, and twist to get into the tightest places so easily.

Amazingly, the life span of this small animal can be up to four years. It can breed at any time and several times a year, and it gives birth to anywhere from five to ten young, which are weaned in three weeks. In two more months, the female can breed again. It has been said that if conditions were perfect, just two mice could produce over 1,000 descendants in a year. Mice that live in houses do not hibernate because of the controlled climate, and thus our house's constant climate perpetuates our mouse problem. Mice will feed on virtually anything from grains and insects to garbage of all sorts, though they prefer vegetable matter. Unlike wild mice, the house mouse stores food only haphazardly.

As a child I was inspired by the story that Walt Disney first thought of Mickey Mouse when a mouse came to visit him in his studio. I didn't know whether that mouse was a common house mouse or a white-footed mouse that had taken up residence in his home, but I was determined to befriend both types. My parents didn't let me keep very much of my nature collection of skulls, skins, arrowheads, and so forth in my bedroom, so I was given a small room for that purpose in the basement. Fortunately, I could do anything I wanted in that room. I could do taxidermy work, clean skulls, keep animal collections, and a whole host of other things best done indoors. For several months I tried feeding the basement mice population, but none would show itself long enough for me to directly feed it. After months of diligent effort, I finally gave up and stopped feeding them altogether, figuring they could forage on their own.

One day while working on piecing together a turtle shell, I was visited by a common house mouse. It was an older one that I called white-face, because of a little streak of white on its face. It boldly crawled up on the table and stood in front of me for a few moments. I paid no attention and didn't stop what I was doing. A few more moments passed and it sat up on its hind legs and gave a good squeak, then another. Reaching into the drawer, I pulled out some seeds and set them down very close to my hand. Without hesitation the mouse began to feed. Within a few minutes, more mice showed up and I kept the handouts coming until I had seven mice feeding all over my table. This relationship went on for years, generation after generation, until the day I brought in a small weasel that had been wounded and kept him in a terrarium till he recovered. The mice were never seen again, even though the weasel could not get out of the terrarium.

Norway rat (*Rattus norvegicus*)

My first encounter with the Norway rat was one I shall never forget. I have since had close encounters with wild dogs, bears, wolverines, criminals, and all manner of ill-tempered beasts, but nothing can match the utter fear that I encountered the first time I met a common rat. Rick and I were crawling under an old barn, looking for artifacts, such as old glass jars, tools, or anything of interest. The crawl space was littered with junk, cobwebs, boards, dusty straw, and bones of dead animals of all sorts. Suddenly from the corner of the crawl space came a vicious sound, a cross between a hiss and a squeal. At first I thought it was a large animal like a raccoon or opossum, but when we shined our lights on it, we saw it was a large rat, the largest rat I had ever seen.

The rat ran straight at us, driving us back toward the opening as fast as we could go. Once outside, it still followed us, threatening and hissing, scaring me so much that I picked up a board and began to defend myself from its jumps and bites. I hit it repeatedly, trying to drive it off, but it would not give up, until two powerful blows killed it. Even in its dying contortions, it still tried to bite us. I hated killing it, but I had to defend myself. From that point on, I have had a healthy respect for the persistent ferociousness of rats. Since then, I have heard of them ganging up on and killing young pigs, sheep, and even calves. In the cities they bite babies and people and spread all manner of disease. They can be repulsive animals, but they are worthy of study as an integral part of our city fauna.

The Norway rat is usually brown, but it can be various shades from lighter to darker almond browns. It can grow to about nine inches long and have up to an eight-inch, virtually hairless tail. The average weight is about a pound but I have seen them much bigger where the food is good and their predatory enemies are few. Normal-size cats can't be considered one of the rat's chief predators, because most full-grown rats can easily fight them off. Even stray dogs have trouble killing a rat, though the feral dogs of the city have a knack for a quick and easy kill, in much the same way a wolf kills a ground squirrel.

Rats can mate at anytime of the year, and a litter averages six young. They can have up to six litters a year, depending on the environmental effects of food availability and conditions. A rat usually becomes sexually mature in two months and is considered old at three years. During certain survival outings when I was forced to live near a large town or city, I frequently caught rats in my traps. Following the laws of the Creator, to let nothing go to waste and to kill nothing in a survival situation needlessly, I have eaten rat. Ironically, I have found them actually quite tasty and I am glad for the experience, since there are many cultures that eat rat regularly. In catching and eating rats you run the risk of disease carried by their fleas but rats trapped away from densely populated areas tend to be cleaner, relatively disease free and much safer to eat.

House sparrow (*Passer domesticus*)

The house sparrow is probably one of the most common smaller birds of our cities and towns. Like any bird of our parks, playgrounds, and streets, they are easily tamed, and in a matter of no time can be eating out of your hand. Introduced into this country in the 1850s, it has proliferated all across our towns, cities, suburbs, and rural areas. It is a hearty little bird, able to withstand many a harsh environment, including that of cities. Since they will eat almost anything and are aggressive, in the country they present fierce competition to many of our natural birds.

They will gang up on birds that are in competition for their feeding and housing needs, thus driving away many of our native songbird species, just as the starling has been driving off our native bluebird. I have even witnessed house sparrows driving off pigeons.

The house sparrows of our cities are not usually as colorful as those that live in the country towns and farms. The city sparrows are a dingy gray with hardly any distinguishing markings. This is due to coloration adaptation to the city environment as well as the soot and dirt picked up from dust and exhaust. The male sparrow has a black throat, white cheeks, and a chestnut nape, while the female is dull brown above and a dirty white beneath. The length of the sparrow is about six inches, the wingspan is just over nine inches, and its tail can be up to 2½ inches.

It nests in any place that affords protection from the elements. It will nest under eaves, in old drain spouts, in abandoned structures, and under bridges. The nest is usually a bulky mass of fibers, grasses, string, bits of trash, and even feathers. They lay four to eight eggs, which have grayish (or reddish or dark brown) spots and which hatch within two weeks.

Pigeon (*Columba livia*)

The more formal name of the pigeon of the cities is rock dove. Before there were such things as cities, these doves lived in Old World rock outcroppings (like those of the Palisades along the Hudson River), where they built their nests and reared their young. Today, the rock dove of the city has adapted to building its nests, roosting, and living on buildings, under bridges, or in locations that have similarities to rock outcroppings.

Over the years there has been so much interbreeding of species that it is difficult to find the ancestral rock-dove coloration of gray body, white rump and dark tail tip. The color patterns of pigeons are varied, from bluish gray to reddish-brown to black bodies, with variously colored wing bars and bands of white. Living in my barn are many rock doves, and typically no two are the same coloration, even those from the same brood. There is said to be some 200 species of pigeons known today, with possibly even more to come as people continue to experiment with crossbreeding. The pigeon's preferred food is grains, but in the cities it will forage the sidewalks and garbage areas for any type of food. Pigeons are easily tamed to take food right from your hand. Many people and communities discourage the feeding of pigeons because of the mess their droppings make on buildings and on statues.

Young pigeons are born blind. For the first several days they are fed what is called pigeon milk, a thick milky secretion from the crop of both parents. After that, they are fed regurgitated grains. In four weeks the young will reach their maximum size, in about six weeks they will molt, and in about nine to eleven weeks they will learn to fly. Some pigeons have been known to live longer than fourteen years.

To practice your stalking ability in the city, the pigeon makes an excellent challenge. They are very deceptive; they will appear to be taking no notice of your presence and will allow you to get very close, only to run or fly off the moment before you can touch them. To touch a pigeon demands a great deal of concentration, knowledge of the bird's habits, and total disregard for what the local populous thinks of your actions. If you have enough time and patience and make sure the bird is distracted by feeding, you can touch your first pigeon.

The reintroduction of the peregrine falcon, a natural predator of the pigeon, is beginning to affect the pigeon population. Many pigeons are developing the evasive habits that were once necessary to avoid peregrines near rock outcroppings.

House finch (*Carpodacus mexicanus*)

Though not as frequently seen in our cities as the house sparrow, but sometimes seen with it, is the house finch. Its habits differ slightly from the house sparrow, so there is a minimum of bickering and vying for territory. The house finch is a wilder species, more displaced in the cities, coming only infrequently and then going on its way like many other migratory birds. The house finch generally likes to nest in sages, mahogany trees, and brush thickets but will also nest around buildings and houses. To the untrained eye, you may think that the house finch is just another sparrow, but upon closer inspection it stands apart easily.

The house finch is about 5½ inches long. The female, smaller and a bit more timid, is a streaked gray and brown and is sometimes hard to distinguish from sparrows, except by its thicker, stouter bill. The male has a pinkish throat and rump, a line over its eye, a back lightly streaked brown and gray and heavily streaked tail and wings. Its belly is grayish. Generally, the nests are built within a short distance to water. The nests are a shallow cup of grass, sometimes containing hair, string, wool, or any soft fiber. The eggs, usually three to six, are bluish or greenish-white with spots of black or brown.

The diet of the house finch is mostly vegetal but very little commercial grains. They prefer thistle, dandelion, and sunflower seeds but sometimes will eat serviceberries, mulberries, and even cherries. Many other grains are on their menu and some finches will readily take handouts in city parks. The house finch is just one of the many kinds of birds you may find living in the city on a temporary basis, especially during the migration time. The sighting of any type of bird should not surprise the city birdwatcher, especially near the abandoned areas, the shorelines, and the parks. In my experience with birdlife in cities, the rule is that any bird is possible.

Mallard (*Anas platrhynchos*)

The mallard is one of the most common ducks of our city ponds and waterways. It sometimes becomes so used to people that it loses much of its fear and can be hand-fed. Many mallards will breed, raise their young and spend most of their lives in the confines of a small park pond. These mallards depart only if the pond freezes solid and handouts become scarce. Even then they will not venture very far, probably only to the next unfrozen body of water, to return again when their original pond thaws and food becomes accessible there. However, some do migrate or are driven off by the stronger ducks because the pond cannot support the population.

Ducks, especially those used to people in city parks, are easy marks for the practicing stalker. They tend to be even easier to stalk than the pigeon, though they can deliver a nasty pinching bite if cornered. Do not let the docileness of the typical city-pond mallards fool you into believing that the wild mallards are just as tame. On the contrary, wilder mallards are quite skittish and will take to the air with the approach of a person. During the migrating season you can always tell which ducks were raised in the wild, which were raised on farm ponds, and which were raised in city ponds by the varying degrees of friendliness toward people. It is my finding that any duck that migrates—whether a few miles or many—will become overly cautious, which is probably due to the effects of hunting seasons along their route.

The mallard was the first duck Rick and I stalked using the floating-blind method. We would choose a pond that had feeding ducks, and set about wrapping weeds around our heads and darkening our faces and necks until it looked like our heads were entirely composed of vegetation. We would then enter the water, walk on the bottom and keep our heads above water to imitate the bits of debris, floating logs and sedges that are always found on ponds. Some Native Americans used to use this method stalking when hunting duck. When close enough they would pull it underwater to break its neck. Because it was normal for a duck to go below the water surface to feed, the other ducks wouldn't be alarmed.

Rick and I weren't hunting ducks to kill but rather to get close enough to them to reach underneath and give them a pinch. This not only made the ducks more aware but also gave us the training we might need if we found ourselves in a survival situation and had to use the same method for food. That afternoon Rick and I had great success touching the ducks, but on my way back to shore, I failed to notice a young female following me, and when I stopped to get through some weeds, she climbed on my head, probably thinking it was a good nesting sight. I jumped with surprise and she bit me right on the forehead, leaving a long-lasting and painful bruise. Grandfather said that it was the duck's way of getting me back for pinching them all day.

The average mallard's length is about twenty-eight inches, including a four- or five-inch tail and a 2½-inch bill. Its wingspan can be up to forty inches and its weight can reach four pounds. The female is smaller than the male and has a predominantly brown color and a purple wing bar. The male, or drake, has a green head and neck, which ends in a white collar bar. The male's breast is purple-brown; the body colors blend from brownish-black to gray and blue; and the tail has an upperward curl.

The nest of the mallard is hidden near water, usually in a thicket of water weeds. The center of the weeds are depressed, and the eggs are laid on the ground. There can be up to twelve eggs, which vary from greenish to a grayish brown in color. Incubation usually takes about twenty-six to twenty-nine days, and the young ducklings, which are a yellowish, downy color, soon learn to walk and swim. The female rears the young and protects them, warning them of danger with a series of calls and utterings. The food of the mallard includes mosquito larvae, grain, and aquatic vegetation such as pickerelweed, arrowhead, and bulrush.

Feral dog (*Canis familiaris*)

No city or large town would be complete without its assortment of feral dogs. These are not stray dogs temporarily loose or lost from their owners; they are, for all intents and purposes, wild dogs. At the outer edges of the Pine Barrens where I was raised, there were dumping grounds that had quite a few feral dogs. Many times there I was treed by dogs and in a few cases badly bitten. Many people encounter feral dogs in the woods and around the outskirts of towns, and many are bitten every year, some killed, by packs of feral dogs that roam the dump areas at will. Some feral dogs even run game animals and do great damage to live-stock. In some states during hunting season, if a dog in the woods appears wild or is running deer, it is legal to shoot it.

Fortunately, the feral dogs of the city are a secretive lot, pre-ferring the seclusion of abandoned areas, old buildings, or dumping areas. Many of these are descendants of dogs that have run wild for generations. They are relatively harmless, unless threatened, but those in a pack (which never numbers more than several) will defend their young. The dogs can be of various sizes, and as in the wolf packs, there are alpha males and females that loosely control the comings and goings of the pack and maintain dominance at the top of a pecking order.

Feral dogs do not usually hunt in packs but a few individuals will wander together. They forage the garbage areas and know where and when the best pickings will be found. Their habits are nocturnal and they stay as far away from human contact as possible. They will catch and kill almost any small game, such as a cat, rat, mouse, or pigeon. They will roam the dock areas and pick up carrion and dead fish, and they will even raid the garbage cans of our city parks.

During the day they den up in abandoned, well-protected, and secluded buildings, culverts, wrecked Dumpsters, or any place they can avoid man. Because of my interest in these feral city dogs and their utter secretiveness, I make it a point to seek them out whenever I am in a city. On one of my long book tours, which consisted of twenty-eight cities in twenty-seven days, I found feral dogs in twenty-two cities, and in those where none were seen, I did find signs of their presence, such as scent posts and numerous tracks in abandoned areas. In New York City by the abandoned piers, I had the privilege of watching a small pack of nine dogs foraging garbage, flotsam, and rats. I carefully followed them into a dilapidated pier and found their den in a small area under the flooring. I could clearly hear the squealing of several pups, probably no more than four weeks old. The alpha male was a larger dog, part collie, part malamute, with a little rottweiler thrown in for good measure. This male was always watchful whenever the pack ate. Anytime a car came by or someone wandered from a waterfront tavern, the pack slipped away into the shadows, only to return when the alpha howled the coast was clear.

Carp (*Cyprinus carpio*)

When Rick and I were children learning the techniques of survival, the carp, in addition to the catfish, was one of our most important teachers. Grandfather would take us to a shallow lake that had been so overrun with carp for years that there were

hardly any other type of fish living there. At that lake we practiced methods for catching fish for hours. First we practiced with
bow and blunt-tipped fish arrow until we got our mark down to
perfection in the refracted angles of the water. With the blunt tip,
the fish weren't killed. Next, we learned to throw and thrust the
fish spear, again with a blunt end, till our mark became precise in
all kinds of water conditions. When we passed the tests and could
hit our fish, we then learned to used barbed and sharpened spears
with great accuracy, in order to be able to feed ourselves in
survival conditions. Eventually, we learned how to stalk the carp
like a heron, and to slowly move our hands over its gill area and
strike and lift the fish from the water bare-handed.

Grandfather told us that we should be caretakers of the earth
and correct the sins of our fathers. That we have allowed an
indiscriminate proliferation of carp is one of those sins. Like the
house sparrow and starling, the carp, which was introduced to our
waters by man, rapidly became overabundant killing off many of
our native fish, and in the process set off events that were
destroying whole ponds and waterways. We used every fish we
caught, just as the laws of nature dictated, and catching the carp
became a beginning step in learning, from which we moved on to
more difficult fish to trap, spear, and net during survival situations. Yes, the carp has a right to be there, but we put them there,
and now have to control them or our waterways will become
barren.

At first glance the carp appears to be a huge goldfish or a big
husky minnow. The carp was introduced into many of our cities'
ponds and waterways, along with goldfish, sunfish, and bass.
Unfortunately, the carp usually comes out on top and ends up
being the dominant fish in the pond. Carp forage by bulldozing
their way through the mud. In the wake of their blundering,
bullish feeding method, they destroy the nests and eggs of other
fish, plow up the vegetation, and generally wreak havoc on the
pond or waterway ecosystem. Carp feed on small fish, small
aquatic plants, mollusks, crustaceans, and other animals strained
from the muck of the water bottom. A feeding carp can be
detected many feet away by the huge plume of sediment it leaves
behind as it feeds.

Carp have coarse, large scales, yet their flesh is soft to the touch. Their back is dark-colored, fading to golden or brown sides. Around the carp's mouth are four distinct barbels, or projections, which aid in feeding and feeling. The dorsal fin extends over almost half of the back. The average carp can grow to fifteen inches long, but much larger carp have been caught, some phenomenally large, from thirty pounds to a record forty-two.

Most of the carp's feeding and breeding is in relatively shallow water. At times you can see at least a third of the back of the fish protruding from the water as it goes about erratically feeding. The carp breeds in late spring, and the female lays up to an estimated two million eggs, which hatch after six to ten days, if environmental conditions are conducive. Unlike other fish, the carp parents do not protect their young. A carp will usually mature in two years if conditions are favorable. Whether you think the carp is a good or bad fish, it is a lot of fun to catch, either on a conventional fishing pole or with more primitive methods. For any angler a carp can put up a good fight, and I personally like the flesh, even though some people wouldn't eat carp if they were starving.

Green heron (*Butorides virescens*)

In the fields, waste places, and waterways of our city parks and playgrounds lives the green heron, a secretive wading bird, much smaller than the great blue heron. The green heron has always been an alluring, mysterious bird for me because of the way it blends in so perfectly with its surroundings. Whether on a city pond or a secluded river basin of a wilderness area, its coloration and slow, secretive movements help it escape detection by even some of the best observers. The green heron was another teacher to Rick and I when we were young children under Stalking Wolf's tutelage. As we did with the great blue heron, we would watch the green heron carefully to learn its slow and exacting stalking movements. But the green heron had far more to teach us than the great blue heron.

The green heron taught us a different stalking step, a way of perfecting our balance while working our feet through the tightest and most tenacious brush. And the green heron taught us how to initiate its utter stillness and patience, and its excellent camouflage, which blended in with almost every place it went. With its stalking behavior and its almost imperceptible motions, it could stalk and catch a wide variety of animals with little trouble. Truly, the green heron is one of the master stalkers and well worth many hours of study.

When visiting city parks or waterways, especially where there are brushy areas, look closely for the green heron. At first it may appear to be an old log sticking from the water, but if you watch, the log will move, cautiously, slowly, and precisely as it stalks game in the water. Even in scant brush, low grasses, small rock outcroppings, or driftwood, the green heron escapes detection. It is as adept at catching animals in the marsh and field as it is in the water. Sometimes when fishing the deeper waters, it will cock its head, readying for the lightning strike, then plunge into the water bodily to catch its prey by spearing it.

The green heron is about seventeen inches long, with short yellow or orange legs that appear too short for a heron. When alarmed, threatened, or annoyed, it will lift its shaggy crest in a beautiful display. Its crown and back is greenish black, with a light line below the eye. Its neck is a deep rufous, which blends into an ash-colored belly. The young birds' necks have black streaks.

The food of the green heron is a variety of insects and small animals, including grasshoppers, crickets, fish, snakes, worms, and even small mammals and frogs. The best time to watch the green heron feeding is in the late evening or very early morning, especially when the mists are thick and it thinks that it is well camouflaged. I find that misty times are some of the best to observe wildlife, because the mists camouflage you and cause the animals to become a little careless.

The green heron's nest, which may be alone or in scattered colonies, is a platform of loose sticks in low trees and shrubs usually located near water and rarely in the woods. Nests are normally from three to eight feet off the ground, but they may be found as high as twenty or more feet. There are usually three to six eggs in a nest, and sometimes two females will use the same nest. The eggs are a beautiful pale blue, and incubation usually takes about twenty days. A short time after hatching, the young will crawl from the nest, using feet and beak, and stand on the branches of the brooding tree. Many lose their footing, fall to the ground and become prey to predators that search beneath the trees for fallen fledglings.

Feral cat (*Felis catus*)

Of the many types of feral cats, those that have once been domestic are the ones usually caught by the local dog catchers. The cats that have never lived with people, that have learned to avoid man, and that have interbred for many generations make up the largest numbers of feral cats found in our cities. Like the feral dogs, they hole up in out-of-the-way places, but they never form packs like the dogs. Usually, only three or four cats will sleep together in a common den, which may be found in old buildings, culverts, trash heaps, or near the local dumping ground. Because they are usually nocturnal and will live close to people yet avoid them whenever possible, they create an aura of mystery. They can live closer to man than feral dogs, because their ability to escape detection by stealth and camouflage is far better than that of the wild dogs, and because they have the ability to climb and thus find safer sleeping and hiding areas near man.

Among feral cats, there is a pecking order, and it is not uncommon for groups of cats to establish territories. Sometimes, disputes occur over the boundaries of these territories, and newly escaped or abandoned domestic cats are sometimes killed if they wander into a group's well-established territory. Even though feral cats will run from man, if cornered they will put up a fierce fight and can inflict some nasty wounds. Diseases among feral cats and dogs can be widespread if too many live in the same area.

Feral cats are not considered a menace to society, mainly because they help to control rodents. I find that the feral cats will eat far less garbage and carrion than the feral dogs. They are very skilled at taking live game like rats, mice, squirrels, and various roosting or feeding birds. They breed at any time of the year, and sometimes several times, if food and conditions are adequate for the care of their young. Though they will not raid the garbage areas as readily as the feral dogs, they will frequent these areas to catch the rodents that are feeding on the garbage. Feral cats have feeding circuits that take them into garbage areas and parks, down sewers, and along the waterfronts.

On several occasions, in various cities, I have noted feral cats migrating from one area to another as the availability of food changed. During these migrations the disputes between competing cat groups reaches a peak, especially during the major migration times of early winter and midspring.

I locate the beds and dens of feral cats with my nose. In poking around abandoned buildings and garbage areas, you will notice the characteristic acrid "spray" odor with which a cat marks his territories. Once located, these areas can be studied from afar but don't be surprised if it takes days to see a feral cat for any den or bed area can have many exits.

Herring gull (*Larus argentatus*)

The common herring gull is one of the most intriguing of all gulls because of its uncanny ability to survive in many of our cities. I have even seen them in places far from any water. On the farm in Asbury, New Jersey, where I conduct my wilderness classes, it is not uncommon to see the farm fields covered with herring gulls foraging for food and water, especially during storms or after the field has been harvested. They dwell around many of our large cities in great abundance, however, mainly because these cities are built near large bodies of water, and because, being scavengers, they are attracted to city dumping sites.

The herring gull is about twenty-six inches long, with a wingspan of fifty-four to sixty inches. The tail is about seven inches long and the bill's length is about 2½ inches. The female is smaller than the male. Both have a grayish back; white head, tail, and underparts; black wingtips; and light beige colored legs. The young birds are brownish with a dark tail the first year, a mottled brown with a whitish tail the second.

Herring gulls will eat just about anything. They relish the garbage dumps of man and pick carrion from beaches. Sometimes they will scoop up live fish and animals from the water surface, and they will eat the eggs and young of nesting shorebirds.

When I was a child in my little hometown located on the Toms River in New Jersey, I saw many types of gulls fly up and down the river in search of food. During one of my walks I found a herring gull with fishing line wrapped around both its legs and the heavy lure impaled in the foot webbing. With the help of Grandfather, Rick and I freed the gull of the tangle, carefully removed the hook, and nursed the gull back to health. Every day, to feed the gull, we would catch shiners with a throw net, until one day it took off without warning. Weeks later I was sitting and fishing at the end of an old dock when a herring gull landed on a piling a few feet from me. It called once, then hopped down beside me, eyeing me and my bucket of bait. The scars on its feet confirmed that it was the gull we had saved. Showing no fear, it took the scraps of bait from my bucket till the supply was exhausted, then it flew off. On several other occasions through that summer and the next, the gull and I would meet at that same dock and it would eat all my bait.

If you have enough patience and time, you can train city herring gulls to feed right from your hands. Gulls seem to recognize and will flock to people who feed them on a regular basis, but it takes a lot of patience to get a gull to take food from your hand. If you try it, be careful, because a gull can deliver a nasty bite, and some carry infections on their bills.

PART III:
THE COUNTRY

Beyond the urban and suburban sprawl lies the country—an assortment of old fields, farmland, country homes and gardens, forests, and waterways. Every city is bordered by country areas, and in less than an hour city dwellers can be in these natural settings. Even though the country is not a true wilderness area, you will find wildlife and plants in abundance there. These areas, more accessible and convenient than wilderness areas, afford great opportunities for nature study, collecting, stimulation and relaxation. The country is the border area between civilization and true wilderness, and is full of adventures, excitement, and endless possibilities for exploration.

Because of the richer variety of landscapes found in the country—transition, second-growth, and farmland areas that create good cover and forage for a wide range of animals and plants—one can often spot more wildlife in the country than in the wilderness. You won't find the larger and more dramatic wild animals, nor those that prefer to be far away from human habitats, but you will find a tremendous abundance.

Unlike the wilderness areas, which are publicly owned, the country is mostly privately owned, excepting state parks, wildlife refuges, and public gamelands. Remember to get the owner's permission—in writing if possible—before you explore private property. If you are conscientious, and respectful of the landscape, there are very few landholders who will not let you use their property. Many fine friendships have been formed between the landholder and the naturalist, and many landholders will even permit you to camp on their grounds for long periods of time.

FIELDS, TRANSITION AREAS, FORESTS

In the country you will find more wildlife in places where there are both fields and forests and transition areas between them. Seek out these places first, for they will be the most rewarding, giving you an opportunity to watch the comings and goings of many different animals that use all of the field-transition-forest areas in their daily routines, to understand their relationships to the land, and to study them individually if you wish.

A frosty dawn enlivens the fall colors as the night slowly drifts into day, as the wash of moisture dazzles the countryside and mists cling to the lowlands, causing the nearer lines of tree to stand out in bold relief and the distances to slowly drift out of focus into obscurity. The symphony of birdsong increases in intensity as the sun slowly warms the frost to dew and brings the landscape to life. Deer drift in and out of shadowy mist, as they slip back to their day beds, while owls, foxes, coyotes, raccoons, and predators and prey of all types seek the shelter of the brush tangles and deeper forest recesses.

As the last patches of mist dry from the landscape and warming air begins to rise, hawks and turkey vultures begin to drift across the sky in search of food. Crows' calls to each other blend beautifully with the other birds' songs, while the call of male pheasants pierce the symphony with their sharp cries. The ebb and flow of music indicates the wanderings of predators that are searching for food, creating the disturbances and alarm calls that echo across the landscape. Adding to the overall symphony are the barks, grunts, squeals, and rustlings of myriad mammals. At once, there is so much to see and so much to listen to, and there are so many questions and so many mysteries to be unraveled.

As the morning wears into afternoon the birdsong drops off slightly, and the landscape quietens as most predators go to sleep. Only the smaller birds, and a few crows, turkey vultures, hawks, and migrating geese can be heard or seen. Mice and voles still scurry through the transition areas, and a few cottontails feed near their beds, but even these activities are few and far between. The drop in the overall animal movement and sound is due to the heat and brightness of the day, the time when most animals are more vulnerable. The hush continues till later in the afternoon when the sun begins to cast long shadows and the lessening of light provides better cover for animals. They stir but stick to the shadows and hollows, awaiting the dark. Birdsong increases with the setting sun, then suddenly melts to a soft silence. Soon the landscape comes alive again with the sound of mammals rustling their way to the various feeding grounds. The symphony increases for a while but then fades as the night approaches midpoint. Again it increases in volume and sound as daybreak nears. At sunrise we experience the greatest music of the day, the loudest and most intense.

As we walk the countryside, so many questions come to mind. What are the jays scolding? What are the sparrows feeding on? Why are the mice squealing? When do the deer bed down? Where does the fox sleep? Why are there so many black cherry trees here but not there? How many raptors, birds of prey, coast across these fields? The questions are endless. There is no fear of running out of mysteries to be solved in this lifetime. With each meandering step, new wonders unfold. There are new discoveries to be made each time you enter the countryside. Everything is changing, evolving, filled with energy and excitement, never staying the same from one moment to the next. Each day something new is to be discovered and studied every step of the way. The country setting is a never-ending source of intrigue and wonder, full of fauna and flora in tremendous abundance.

Because the countryside is so varied and each area contains so many animals and such a wide variety of plants, the best way to explore is to wander, following your heart wherever you go. Certainly a blind can be built, but that is very restricting, and if you limit yourself to a blind, the wealth of wildlife will remain undiscovered. Drifting about the landscape quietly will reward the observer with far more sightings and mysteries. (Stalking will be discussed at length in Part IV.) The country landscape is one that should be wandered over without time or destination. With a few short excursions into the country, you will begin to learn landscapes and their various animal populations and their interdependence.

If you can find a location that has fields that border transition areas, then a blind of some sort would be advisable. A blind can be located to one side of the thicker transition areas, in the beginning line of trees or in a stout tree. It is best to lash the blind to the tree rather than use nails, because with lashing little damage is done. I prefer the tree stand because of the view it affords and its ease of concealment. Very few animals will look up for danger, even those that would be prey for the raptors. If you are using a tree stand, it is advisable to have a safety rope or strap. Any hunting store will have safety straps, and some will have self-supporting tree stands. There are many tree stands on the market that are dangerous, so if you buy one, check with the store owner or with hunters that use stands to make sure that a particular tree stand provides good stability and safety. If you don't want to make your own camouflaging, stores also have camouflage overalls, hats, and gloves, as well as camouflage netting, which will all add to your concealment, whether you are on the ground or in a tree. Scent maskers, such as doe-in-heat or fox-urine, can also be bought at the same stores.

At my farm, where I hold my beginners' survival, tracking, and nature classes, I have blinds at key locations throughout the landscape. I can leisurely drift from one to another and watch all sorts of animals at work and play without them detecting my presence. Sometimes I'll create the call of a dying rabbit or mouse by sucking the back of my hand, which will bring in many predators, such as foxes, coyotes, raccoons, hawks, and weasels. All predators are opportunists and will steal the catch from a smaller or uncareful predator, so the call of an animal in distress will attract many predators that are curious. Another sound you can make that works just as well is twirling the butt end of a feather between your palms, which produces the sound of a thrashing bird. To bring predators near the blind, you can also dangle a feather from a string that is attached to a bush to arouse curiosity.

Abandoned farms are one of my favorite areas for country

exploration. These old farms have fields that have long overgrown, many have small trees and brush tangles. These overgrown fields provide good cover, food variety, and environment
for all manner of birds, reptiles, and mammals, both predator and
prey. Abandoned farm buildings provide good nesting, roosting,
and bedding sights for many other animals, including barn owls,
house sparrows, finches, barn swallows, skunks, weasels, rats,
mice, opossums, raccoons, and many many others. Old farms
offer endless possibilities for exploration and also afford some of
the best environments for wildflowers of many types.

WATER AREAS

The presence of a body of water increases a country area's abundance of wildlife. Streams and lakes are best explored by wandering along the banks. The wildlife of ponds and small lakes are best
observed by utilizing a blind or a tree stand in the thickest
vegetation of the waterway. A rowboat, canoe, or kayak is a good
way to explore many of the waterways. Because these boats are
relatively quiet and mask, to some degree, human scent it is
possible to drift right up to a deer or other animals along the
bank. Submerging yourself and using a face mask and snorkel can
increase your chances of sneaking up on fish, turtles, snakes,
deer, and many other animals, since the water provides a natural
blind. I sometimes camouflage my head with mud and weeds,
then silently drift down to watering deer and get close enough to
touch them.

The surface of the pond reflects the dawn sky. With the increasing intensity of the sun, the frogs begin to sing again and
insects begin to stir. Bank, barn, and tree swallows begin to
wheel and coast above the surface, skimming the water for a drink
or darting after an insect. The waters stir now and then with a
feeding bass or sunfish, with turtles and snakes slipping in and
out. A belted kingfisher hovers above the shimmering surface,
then, in an instant, plunges in after a small chub sucker, and in
the shadows of the vegetation a little green heron stalks small

sunfish and frogs. Everywhere along the banks are mud-inbedded tracks of mammals and birds. Each track is a word, and each set of tracks is a story of a foraging or drinking animal. Even the tracks of small insects and other invertebrates, as well as salamanders and reptiles, can be seen and studied. The mud bank of a waterway is one of the best places to learn how to track.

Bodies of water are among my favorite places in the natural world, especially swamps, estuaries, and small ponds. Life around the waterways is nothing less than intense and dramatic. In this most prolific of natural environments, there is always something going on, some animal about, and hosts of plants to study. Most larger animals, those that don't get enough water from succulent plants, animals, or dew-rich browse, must come to drink at one time or another. Within a short period of observation, more wildlife can normally be spotted in a water area than in any other area.

The Native American peoples looked at the waters as being the blood of Earth Mother. To them it was a sacred entity, the lifeblood of all things. To defile the waters in any way was nothing less then a sacrilege. Many ceremonies utilized water, either as a sacred symbol in the ceremony itself or as a setting for the ceremony. They could plainly see how all things depended on water for survival. The waters were strengthening, soothing, and cleansing—a precious gift to all life. The Native Americans zealously took care not to waste or pollute the waters and were appalled at the way the settlers took water for granted or polluted it. Today, we must learn anew what water means to the earth, the animals, the plants, and us. Most of our water sources are polluted beyond correction, and we may soon run out of fresh water.

To lay back against the bank of a stream or on a small hill overlooking a swamp is to enjoy the most comfortable place on earth. All natural elements seem to combine there. The waters take on many moods, and the mists always add a sense of magic. To be sure to see a wide range of wildlife in the country, seek out the water areas first, sit for a while, and watch the tremendous show of nature unfold in front of you. Simply stated, water areas and transition areas afford the most variety of all the landscapes.

SEASHORES

Many of our cities and suburbs border oceans, and the seashores are widely visited by vacationers, especially during the summer. The little strip of beach and dune buffering the houses from the waves is a wilderness in itself. Even on the busiest beaches there is always something fascinating to discover. Shorebirds scavenge along the surf's edge for food, and at night after the human crowds have left, mammals and other shore life come to forage live food or raid garbage cans.

In the early morning, after the tides have washed the beaches clean of human prints and when the castings of the ocean wash up new mysteries, is the best time to search the beaches for clues of what went on during the night. The beaches are covered with animal tracks and treasures cast up by the tides. Any small patch of shells can be a source of hours of exploration and absolute fascination. The hours seem to slip away as you discover and collect the tiniest shells, stones, and other marine forms washed up by the waves. Many people look for and collect the grand conch shells and other large treasures, but if you narrow your gaze to the smaller things, you will fill your collecting bags in no time at all. The shapes, colors, and textures of the shells and driftwood defy description. Among the drift castings are myriad tracks of a huge assortment of shore animals. Winding in random patterns, like a delicate tapestry, the tracks leave clues to the animal's identity and actions.

From sunrise to the time the beaches become crowded is also one of the best times to watch beach wildlife. That is the time when many of the shorebirds are most active. The predawn is the best times to see mammals and other night-active shore life.

The beach is a mystical storehouse of never-ending excitement, adventure, new discovery, and countless treasures. If people would only stop long enough from their suntanning and swimming, they would discover a realm of fascination that would bring out the child in all of them.

The sea itself, besides what it offers us in marine life and recreation, is a grand source of stimulation. It has many moods and as many faces. Careful observers can learn to interpret signs of upcoming weather systems, fish movements, and ocean conditions for the next day. Reading the sea, which can change in a breath of wind from dead calm to violent pounding surf, is a science in itself, as many an old sailor will tell you. It has also been an inspiration to poets, writers, philosophers, painters, photographers, and lovers since the dawn of time and will continue to be as long as man has the foresight to not pollute it into a caldron of sickening chemical wastes.

To the human spirit, water, especially moving water, and most especially the ocean, has a deep, soothing effect. That is why so many of us seek the beaches for rejuvenation, for play, for relaxation, and for introspection. The more we learn about the seashore—one of the most alluring of all wild places—and the more we explore it, the more we will understand the sea—one of the mightiest forces on the face of earth.

ANIMAL LIFE

Coyote (*Canis latrans*)

I admire the coyote because of the way it has expanded its range to most of this country and because of the ease with which it eludes and blends in with mankind, despite the bounty it still has on its head in many states. The coyote's elusiveness and adaptability has made it all but invisible to most people—even many wildlife authorities.

The coyote has continued to expand its range from west to east across our country. It seems to proliferate wherever man is, and the more we try to kill it off, the more coyotes we seem to end up with. The government and private ranchers have tried poisoning, trapping, and shooting them, but coyotes still increase in numbers.

In my travels I have noticed many coyotes of different sizes, colorations, and habits. In the warmer southern climates coyotes tend to be quite small, while the more northern coyotes are quite large. They can be secretive, quiet, true masters of the shadows, knowing that their very survival depends on how well they elude mankind. Or they can be bold and boisterous, especially in the out-of-the-way areas and where man is not in hot pursuit. I believe that the coyote's ability to adapt quickly to new environments and conditions is the cause of its proliferation.

Grandfather held the coyote in the highest regard, as an animal almost as spiritual and powerful as the eagle. While some Native American tribes thought of the coyote as the trickster and a little foolish, Grandfather considered it a trickster, too, but also a very intelligent and revered teacher. The early childhood of Rick and I was filled with Grandfather's parables and tales of the adventures of coyotes as teachers. Grandfather considered himself a coyote teacher—a teacher who, while teaching you one thing, would also teach you many others, and prepare you for future lessons and experiences. To this day I am still learning lessons from the coyote. I hold the coyote in the highest regard, for, as most of my survival students will confirm, I, too, am a coyote teacher.

The first time Rick and I saw a coyote in the Pine Barrens, we were seated at the edge of a field on a richly moonlit night. Though the spring grasses were closely cropped, they were still tall enough to give cover to the smaller animals like mice and rabbits and we sat there waiting for predators, such as owls or foxes. The night was alive with a thousand voices of insects and frogs and the rustlings of many animals, prey and predator alike. A few owls hovered like huge moths over the outer edge of the field but none had yet dropped; a gray fox pounced on a patch of grass, then wandered off with what seemed to be a small vole. It was a good night for predators, for the field at this time of year was prolific with wildlife and a favored hunting ground, and the moon made the entire field look like a dimly lit stage.

At the far end of the field a fox, or what we thought to be a fox, entered and glanced cautiously around. As it stepped into the full moonlight, we observed that it was larger, longer and lighter in color than the gray fox we had seen earlier, and it was walking, moving, and hunting far differently. Then we thought it might be a small dog, but because of its movement, its stealthy way of hunting, its longer snout and large ears, we quickly abandoned that idea. We glanced at Grandfather and saw a wide grin appear on his face. No words passed between us, but we knew that we were witnessing our first coyote. We watched its every move for over half an hour till it disappeared quietly, slipping first to the edge of the field, then finally disappearing into the shadows. It made no noise either coming or going, and even its killing of the voles and mice was done silently and effectively.

Grandfather explained also that few people knew—or acknowledged—that there were coyotes in New Jersey, of all places. We tracked the coyote for over a week until we finally arrived at an excavated hole under a fallen pine tree. The hole was small and well hidden, but a group of four pups played just at the entrance. We watched for hours as the coyotes came and went, caring for their family. For the remainder of the summer we watched the pups grow until they began to wander and hunt together and we could no longer silently keep up with their roamings and speed. I was awed by their utter secretiveness and deception, and by the uncanny way they could elude man, dog, trap, and gun.

I was so excited about my find of the coyotes that I took my story to a local biology teacher, who didn't believe that I could even distinguish between a fox and a dog. After showing him the difference in the tracks and some pictures, he would still not believe me. His argument was that he had been wandering around the Pine Barrens for years and had never encountered a coyote. My story met with the same response from the local game wardens and professors at the state college. I began to question how good "book learning" really was. This doubt was probably one of the major factors in my deciding not to go to college, for if "top" biologists could not tell the difference between a dog track and a coyote track, there definitely seemed to be something wrong with the modern college education. I firmly believe that all graduates in the fields of natural history should spend at least two years in fieldwork, learning firsthand from nature's university, without their books or theories or stuffy indoor classrooms. Perhaps mankind has been away from the woods all too long.

The coyote measures about four foot from the tip of the nose to the end of its bushy tail. The average male weighs up to fifty pounds and the average female about thirty pounds, though in the more northern reaches of North America I have seen them both a little longer and heavier. The ears are large and erect, and look as if they are too big for their heads. Most coyotes are a pale brown, dusted with gray, white, or black, giving them, from a distance, and depending on the part of the country you are in, a gray, whitish, or a very pale yellow appearance. The underparts are usually white but the ears seem darker than the overall coloration.

A coyote's normal range is about six miles but that can be smaller in good hunting areas and larger in the poorer ones. It has been said, however, that during migrations or to reach distant hunting areas, a coyote can lope at forty miles an hour for over eight hours.

Coyotes pair for life, though I have noted that a few younger coyotes have switched mates from one season to the next. The usual breeding time is mid to late winter and gestation is a little over sixty days, so the pups are born when the spring is in full bloom and hunting is best. A pup will nurse for about two weeks, and at three to four weeks the pups may be moved to another den. Within six to seven weeks they will begin to run with their parents. Unlike wolves, which stay together in tight family groups for extended periods of time, a coyote family usually stays together only until the late fall, never past the next breeding season. Though many coyotes are killed before they grow very old, they can live ten or more years. In addition to rodents, rabbits, and game, they will eat carrion and almost anything they can find which is why they sometimes raid the garbage areas of our towns.

White-tailed deer (*Odocoileus virginianus*)

One of the animals I hold in the highest regard is the deer. For its size, it is one of nature's most secretive animals, living virtually under people's noses and yet hardly ever being detected. As proof, one only has to look at the local hunting records to compare the relatively low number of deer killed each year with the high number of deer hunters. The deer's uncanny ability to escape observation, to stalk and yet blend with its surroundings helps it, even in more densely populated areas, to survive. Its

senses are acute and will warn a deer of an impending danger
long before the hunter will be aware of the deer's presence. Once
danger is detected, deer escape through intricate trails leading to
the heaviest brush, or they hide in inaccessible areas. If a deer
has a good hiding place, it can remain undetected even if a hunter
passes within a few feet. In fact, a deer will often choose cover
rather than flight, because a fleeing animal is a vulnerable animal.

When Rick and I were first taught to stalk—the art of moving
through the woods silently and unseen—it was the deer that we
sought, even though sighting one seemed an elusive dream, far
out of the reach of our abilities. We tried and tried to touch a
deer but hardly ever got closer than a few feet. Whenever we
would see one feeding in the distance, we would try to stalk it,
and each time we would be able to draw closer before it ran off.
We got so discouraged that we became desperate. We would
spend hours lying camouflaged beside a deer trail in order to have
them walk within a few feet of us. At every available moment we
would study their habits, till we felt we knew them and their
movements intimately. In time we could tell what a deer was
going to do by reading its body language and the series of grunts
that accompanied its actions. Grandfather used to say that the
more we knew an animal, the more we would see it in the
wilderness, and the more adept we would become at stalking it.

One of the more frustrating aspects of tracking deer was simply
trying to find prints in the forest litter. We thought that, since the
deer were big and had hard hooves, they would be easy to track.
We soon learned that despite the hard hooves a deer could pass
through many areas and hardly leave a track. I have a great deal
of respect for the deer people and their ability to escape detection. Many people don't realize that deer live right in their
neighborhood. But over the years I've learned that deer can live
in a wide variety of areas. In no time at all they can adapt to a
new area and stay hidden and safe from people, predators, and
cars. And often I've found deer living in areas where you wouldn't
expect to find them at all, never mind thrive.

Deer are also indicator animals, which means that if an area can
support deer, it will also support a wide assortment of other
animals. That is why I always look for deer signs when I first

approach a new area. As far back as I can remember, deer were important teachers to Rick and I, and we still study the deer today to check our skills.

The first encounter I had with deer came when I was ten years old. For months Rick and I had attempted to track and stalk the deer but could not get within touching distance. The frustration of having a deer run off was enough to make us want to quit at times. But we persevered, attempting all manner of ways to get close to the deer, but none worked very well and those that did, didn't get us as close as we wanted. *Finally*, after months of trial and error, I found a way of stalking that would put me right next to a deer. I found a well-worn trail used by the deer every night. Deadening my scent and camouflaging myself, I lay on the trail replacing an old log that had been there for years. In an hour I could hear the deer coming. My heart started to pound and the excitement grew with each approaching step. Suddenly, the steps stopped just a few feet away, the deer snorted a few times, then ran off. The rest of the evening produced no more deer.

Disgusted with myself, I approached Grandfather and told him about the deer. I knew that I had been well camouflaged and hadn't moved a muscle, but the deer had still detected me and run off. Grandfather asked me if I was also camouflaged inside, but I didn't understand what he was trying to say. He then asked me how I *felt* as the deer approached, and I recounted the excitement. He told me that animals detect each other in ways beyond the physical senses, and that it had been the sensing of my nervousness that had frightened the deer off. I asked him how I could quieten my excitement, and he told me to let go of my mind and *become* a log. The next night I got into the same position and pretended that I was a log. I lay very still, feeling my skin to be bark, my heaviness the log's weight. I was so caught up in pretending that I was a log that I failed to hear the deer coming until they were stepping over me. As the last one started over me, my excitement overflowed; the deer became frightened and stepped squarely on my stomach.

Realizing the far-reaching wisdom of what Grandfather had taught me, I began to imagine myself as a shadow when I was stalking. This change in attitude increased my stalking ability greatly, and within a month I had touched my first deer. Throughout my life the deer have taught me many things, but the wisdom of the inner sense, of communication beyond words, was one of the most dramatic lessons of my life. It seems that the deer's ability to escape detection stems from an ability to sense all the nuances of the landscape in general, much like the catfish can sense where food is by using its tactile barbels.

The size of the white-tail deer, and its relatives—found throughout North America—is determined by the area in which it lives. The larger deer will stand to four foot at the shoulder and will weigh up to 300 pounds. The females are slightly smaller than the males. During the summer months they are a reddish-brown, with a white underside; in the winter they turn a grayish over white. Their coloration blends easily with most landscapes. The antlers of the bucks are forward-pointing with the prongs or tines pointing upward. The fawns are spangled with white spots, much like sun dappling on the forest floor, making them virtually invisible when they are bedded down in leaves.

Deer prefer to live near the transition or fringe areas. These areas of shrubs, brush tangles, vines and forbs make the best feeding areas. Food consists of typical browse, such as twigs and leaves of many plants. Deer breed in the late fall and early winter, and the fawns are born in late spring or early summer, depending on the area. The newborn deer bed down for several weeks but at four to five weeks old they begin to follow their mother. A young doe may stay with her mother for two years, while a young buck only stays with the mother for a year. Typically, a deer will give birth to twins, though only one fawn may be born to younger does and does in areas where there is a lack of food.

Striped skunk (*Mephitis mephitis*)

One of my first encounters with the striped skunk will always be implanted in my mind, or rather my nose. I was camouflaged beside a riverbank, looking at foraging raccoons and hoping one would wander close enough to touch. Touching a raccoon is difficult, not because they are particularly stealthy, but because they will often turn around and bite. My hope was that I could touch a raccoon quickly, then stand up and scare it off before it attacked my hand.

In the distance, over the rush of water I could hear what seemed the typical sound of a pacing raccoon. I did not, however, take into account the pitch darkness nor the similarity between the sound of the walk of the raccoon and that of the skunk. I slipped my hand slowly through the brush toward the dark moving object and the sound of shuffling feet. I tapped what I thought was a raccoon, then stood up to run, only to be sprayed by a frightened skunk. I immediately dove into the cold river and tried to wash off, but to no avail; my eyes stung and the thick odor gave me a violently upset stomach. For days I tried to get rid of the odor, bathing in everything from vinegar to tomato juice, just as the old-timers recommend, but no matter what I did, I just couldn't kill the stench. The smell was so bad that I couldn't stay in a shelter but had to sleep under the stars. Eventually the odor wore off, and I could begin living with myself again. I found out later that Grandfather had any number of plants that would get rid of the scent, but I was too embarrassed at the time to go to him for help.

My apprehension of and respect for skunks has lasted to this day, but I find them fascinating and a rather good teacher. My early experience with the striped skunk has kept me at a distance for quite some time, though I do sometimes study them at close range. Grandfather held the skunk in the highest regard not only because of its protective scent spray, but also because it is a master forager and collector of herbs. When a skunk forages a given area, it leaves no stone unturned, as it were, and will continually grub up the soil in search of a wide variety of foods. In our stalking we would follow a skunk for hours, till it got too dark to see, watching it rip apart old logs, overturn rocks, and rout soil in an asiduous search for food.

Over the years Rick and I learned the habits and body language of the skunk. We knew exactly when they were going to spray and when they were bluffing, enabling us to beat a hasty retreat anytime we made a mistake and aroused a skunk's fear. Generally, when danger approaches, they will sniff the air, holding their muzzles high. Sometimes they will threaten by pounding on the ground with their front feet and hissing loudly. When they are ready to spray, they will turn, lift their tails high and forward, and rock side to side, then forward on their rear feet. At this last point, we learned that there is no retreat, because a skunk can spray up to twenty feet, providing that the wind is right.

During my early childhood a family of skunks lived under our house. Every year I would watch them raise their young and leave with their little family on foraging trips. Though a skunk's life expectancy in the wild is rarely over three years, the oldest female under my house lived for over four. I did get quite friendly with the skunks without ever being sprayed, though I did have some close calls.

Because skunks seem to have poor eyesight and may mistake you for an enemy, I found that it was safer just to sit and wait for them to come to me, rather than trying to stalk them. To get them familiar with my presence, I would sit near their exit hole by the porch. Every few nights I would edge closer and closer, till they were walking within a few inches of me and showed no fear. Though it did take some time before they would accept food from me, eventually I did get the whole family of skunks to eat from my hand.

One should be careful, however, in trying to attract skunks. Once, while in my late teens, I was reaching into a hollow log to see what was there and was bitten by a skunk. Although they rarely bite, they are one of the largest carriers of rabies in the United States and should be approached with the utmost caution. Their spray is bad enough, but because of their needle-sharp teeth, their bite is nasty. The skunk will also sometimes feed on carrion, which makes their bite a possible carrier of infection. Then again, one should be careful of all animals because their bites and scratches could lead to infection or worse.

Skunks can grow to about thirty inches, have a seven-inch tail, and reach 14 pounds (more in captivity). Generally, the striped skunk is black with two white stripes running one on either side of the spine. However, different stripe widths and patterns can be seen, including none at all. With the exception of only a few areas, these animals are found throughout the United States. They mate in late winter or early spring; after last year's young leave. The young are born in a den and will nurse for six to seven weeks, and the male sometimes rejoins family when the young are old enough to leave the den. It is not uncommon for a skunk to use another animal's abandoned den. Skunk families will also stay together through the colder parts of winter for warmth. They feed mainly on insects, fruit, berries, mice, small rodents, carrion, birds, and grains, as well as garbage.

Pygmy shrew (*Microsorex hoyi*)

The shrew people are some of the best and most voracious hunters of the mammal world. Its diminutive size—a shrew weighs just slightly more than a penny—is deceptive. Because it has an extraordinarily high metabolism, with a breathing rate of about 850 times a minute and a similar heart rate, a shrew will eat three to four times its body weight each day. Their sense of hearing is acute, but their eyesight is poor except at short distances. Despite their long snout they have a relatively poor sense of smell, but these handicaps do not hinder the shrews' hunting capability or success.

Grandfather admired the shrew for its hunting ability and lightning-fast reflexes. Rick and I would spend hours on the forest floor studying the shrew people, learning all we could about their hunting and stalking abilities and how nothing in their immediate environment escaped detection. The more I studied the shrew, the more I realized that the animal was not as vicious as is commonly thought. They *will* attack animals much larger than themselves but only when defending themselves or their young. When they do kill, it is not randomly or without cause. Hunting and killing is for food, and because of their insatiable appetites, they must kill and eat often.

I have seen shrews, in defense of their young, kill mice several times their size. The dead mice were eaten, but mice are not usually on the shrew's menu, and a shrew will not attack a mouse under normal conditions. Another time I witnessed a shrew drive off a young weasel, and in another instance two shrews attacked a young house cat. The only time I ever saw a shrew threaten a person was when one of my students inadvertently stumbled onto a shrew's nest. The female shrew, in defense of its young, drove the student away with a series of high jumps and ominous squeals. The student was so shaken that he retreated hastily, defending himself with a stout stick. With each prod of the stick the shrew jumped forward and chased the student. From a distance, the sight of this 200-pound man beating a fast and terrified retreat from the diminutive shrew was rather amusing.

To study the world of the shrew you must learn to look at the earth closely. In the forest-floor realm of the shrew, it is one of the most vicious predators, comparable to a panther in its realm of the jungle. The shrew's world is one of lightning speed and fast living. It is very exciting to watch a shrew stalking through the forest litter for small insects and amphibians. They blend beautifully with their environment, and appear to be but shadows moving silently through the leaf cover or fields.

The shrew can be found throughout the United States in landscapes as varied as country settings and densely populated areas. Just beyond the back door of my boyhood home, at the edge of a small field bordered by thick forests, lived several families of shrews. They led very secretive lives, easily avoiding my family, the dogs, and the cat. Yet every evening they would hunt in our gardens and in the old lumber piles. I would constantly see their prints in the sandy areas or their partially eaten prey.

Over the years I've located quite a few nests with newborns. Some of the older shrews might wander relatively far on their nightly foraging circuits. I tracked one male for more than 100 yards from where it bedded down. I also found that the shrews were active night or day and that they never slept very long but rather took catnaps.

I learned also the viciousness of the slightly poisonous shrew bite. I was calling in owls one night by running my hand through the fallen leaves and squeaking much like a mouse. Somehow a shrew escaped my observation, and it delivered a good bite to my pinky. The bite, though small, swelled my whole hand for a number of days, rendering it useless and causing much pain.

The common shrew is about three inches long with a 1½-inch tail and weighs just slightly over one-tenth of an ounce. The sexes are similar in coloration; a deep brown above, and a gray or buff beneath. The eyes are small and beadlike, and the ears are partially hidden by the thick fur. Shrews favor forest floors and thick overgrown fields where food is plentiful. When they have litters, the females will not tolerate males because males will eat the young. Females give birth about three weeks after breeding to a litter of four to nine, the number depending on food availability; if environmental conditions are conclusive several litters may be produced in one year. Shrews feed on insects, salamanders, worms, and other small animals.

Common mole (*Scalopus aquaticus*)

As children Rick and I went to elaborate measures to study the moles. At first we only saw what most people see, the raised tunnels running randomly through the lawns, fields, and forests. It seemed that to see the moles we should dig up the tunnels, but no sooner did we dig, than the mole would disappear. At best we would only catch a fleeting glimpse; the only ones seen at close range were the ones killed by the cat. Finally I located a well-used tunnel, removed the top and covered it with Plexiglas. On a bright, moonlit night, we could just make out the moles passing beneath the cover. To see better we turned on a flashlight which only sent the moles into the darker, covered, recesses of the tunnels. My dad had us try a red light, explaining that that was what they used during World War II because it wouldn't affect night vision. We tried the red light and it worked splendidly. Several years after that, I had the good fortune of locating a den where young moles were being raised. Carefully digging down beside the den, Rick and I again put in a Plexiglas sheet and were able to watch the newborns for a few nights before the mother moved them.

I have been able to actually touch moles, but the last time I tried I received a bad bite. Sitting for hours with my finger imbedded in their tunnels and my ear close to the ground, I could hear them coming, and they would move by and brush against my finger. I guess that the last time I tried it, the tip of my finger looked too much like a grub—that mole refused to let go until I pulled it out of its tunnel and shook it off.

Grandfather loved the feel of the mole's soft velvetlike fur. He wouldn't trap or hunt moles—because of their small size—but he would use the fur if he happened to find one dead. Using an old Native American method, he would tan the hide and then sew the pelts into medicine bags, in which he would store his medicinal herbs or favorite items. He held the mole people in the highest regard because they were one of the few animals that lived within Earth Mother, which to him was a highly sacred home for any animal. Rick and I learned to connect ourselves to the earth by watching how the mole so completely depended on the earth. The mole is a very powerful teacher and spirit.

The male mole can grow to 7¼ inches long with a 1¼-inch tail. The females are slightly smaller. Their fur is thick, gray and velvety. They have stout claws, spadelike feet for digging, and a naked nose that can be used for probing soils, much like a pick. Their eyes are very small and seedlike. Though moles live underground within intricate and extensive tunnel systems, the adult males will wander overground in search of females during the mating season. Moles will usually breed in March and give birth to four or five young in April. The young become independent by mid May and reach maturity in ten months. Moles will eat earthworms, grubs, insects and insect larvae, and some plant material, though it is only a small portion of their diet.

Red squirrel (*Tamiasciurus hudsonicus*)

The red squirrel is one of our most aggressive little mammals. For its size, it is very strong and very fast, and it will think nothing of chasing off animals many times bigger, or of scolding humans that pass too close to their trees.

I have seen red squirrels drive off or kill gray squirrels, drive away hawks and owls, and harass and foil many predators' attempts at stalking game. In fact, the red squirrel will go as far as throwing pine cones and sticks down on passersby, all the while scolding the intruders with high-pitched whirring sounds. At times the red squirrel can become so fearless that it will actually approach you, threaten you with sounds and feign attack as it edges closer and closer. This behavior can become quite intimidating, and I have seen many people forced to leave a perfectly good blind for fear of being attacked, which rarely ever happens. Despite its being an aggressive bully, the red squirrel can teach us much about bravery, strength, and the benefit of lightning-fast reflexes. It can also teach us much about the joy of play and climbing.

I love to watch the swift antics and powerful gymnastics of the red squirrel. I can sit for hours watching them gather food, communicating with each other, and defending their territory. They seem to have boundless energy and to never tire of playing or testing their strength. They are usually quite intimate and peaceful with their own kind, and for the most part, you will see them playing or relaxing in trees rather than aggressively attacking their surroundings.

However, the day I decided to try to touch one, I pushed my luck too far, which almost resulted in a permanent injury not only to my body but also to my ego. I had been watching a particular red squirrel for a number of weeks and knew the little fellow quite well. It had approached me a number of times, trying to drive me off, but I had refused to yield my ground. We lived in a sort of peaceful coexistence, or perhaps standoff, in which it seemed to accept, or at least tolerate, me as part of the landscape. I knew most of its habits, movements and language quite well, especially its favorite roosts and trails in the tree branches. I had decided to get into a fork of a tree, meet it at the end of one of its branches and touch it. I camouflaged my body and scent to simulate that of the white pine trees in which it lived, and I nestled myself in the tree fork.

I waited there for a long time, watching the red squirrel feed in a distant tree. It began lacing its way through the trees, taking all the branches I expected it to take toward where I was waiting. Everything seemed to be going well until, without warning, it took a side turn and disappeared. Again I waited, but could not see him nor hear him make any noise. Suddenly I caught a reddish flash over my shoulder and the red squirrel delivered a painful bite into my upper shoulder, near my neck. The pain was excruciating and continuous as it sunk its teeth and claws in deeper. Try as I might, I could not shake it off. I lost my balance, and both the squirrel and I fell several feet to the ground.

I was knocked unconscious for some time, and when I awoke, I was covered with blood, my neck badly sprained, and my head pounding. The red squirrel sat only a few feet away, watching me carefully in a seemingly caring manner. Ironically, from that moment on, we became the best of friends. I fed it frequently; it took food from my hand, sat on my knee, and allowed me to pet it. It would even roll on its back and allow me to stroke its belly. I don't know what had produced such a dramatic behavioral change in this feisty little squirrel, but it never showed aggression toward me again. I can only guess that since it defeated me and drove me out of its tree, it no longer saw me as a threat.

Red squirrels are the watchdogs of the forest, warning animals of approaching danger. Many times while tracking various criminals, I have been kept aware of the whereabouts of the quarries by the red squirrel's scolding of them as they walked through the woods. As a tracker, you begin to depend on the sounds of the red squirrel—as well as many other animals and birds—to let you know what is going on in the forest. A call, the repetition of a call and its intensity will tell you exactly what the squirrel, or animal, is scolding, and where it is.

While Grandfather taught us the wisdom of the ancient Apache scouts that enabled them to know where all the animals were on the landscape, the red squirrel became our first animal teacher of this skill. When anything moves in nature, it makes a disturbance and like a stone thrown into a pond, it creates a series of disturbances much like concentric rings across the landscape. The red squirrel often acts as one of these concentric rings. By paying close attention to the squirrels and listening to their scolding of various animals or people, you can easily learn to judge the distance and direction of their voices and thus pinpoint the source and widening effects of the original disturbance. Once the language of the red squirrel is mastered, then it becomes an easy step to learn the language of anything else.

The red squirrel is about twelve inches long, including a 4½-inch tail. Sexes are of similar size and color. In the winter they are a gray-white beneath and a dark reddish brown above, and in the summer they turn white beneath and a brighter red above. They are common everywhere from city parks to the wilderness, though they prefer to live in coniferous forests. They mate in late winter and produce a litter of three to five young that are weaned in five weeks. In some areas they will have two litters a year. The family stays together for the summer, and the life span can be over ten years. The red squirrel will eat all manner of plant and animal matter. Seeds, nuts, fruit, insects and occasionally bird eggs are the main staples of their diet.

Eastern screech owl (*Otus asio*)

My first encounter with the screech owl literally scared Rick and me out of the woods. We were not yet nine years old and not very proficient at camping alone. The woods were still a great mystery and we took great pleasure in scaring each other by telling late-night ghost stories. We were camped about a mile from home beside a swamp we called Turtle Run. That night the swamp grew quite misty and the moon played tag with the rapidly moving clouds. We spooked each other, trading stories of ghosts and weird beasts until neither of us would leave the firelight for firewood. As the night closed in on us, the mist took on shapes, and shadows began moving mysteriously through the trees. It was then that two screech owls began their wailing song and sent us running home. I don't think that I took a breath till I was inside my house, and I know I have never run faster in my life.

The next day we returned to our camp area to collect our things, since we had carried nothing with us on our hasty trip home. Grandfather was in our camp and smiled at us as we walked in. He knew that we had run from the woods, because of our footprints and the way we had left the camp area. After he scolded us for leaving the campfire, he took us on a short hike to the far end of the swamp where a farmer's field adjoined the bottomlands. There at the edge of the field stood an old apple

Screech Owls

tree, gnarled and battered by the years in the poor, pine-rich soils. He sat us down and told us to watch a cavity in the upper trunk. We sat for a long time, till the sun had sunk deep into the horizon. Suddenly a screech owl appeared, gazed knowingly around, then flew to the upper branches of the tree. We were excited because seeing an owl is a rare occurrence.

As Grandfather spoke about the life of this little owl, the quietude of dusk was shattered by the same screaming song that had scared us out of the woods the night before. We jumped to our feet and began to back up, until Grandfather laughed and told us what had made the sound. Once we realized that the sound was made by the screech owl calling its mate—and being reassured by Grandfather's presence—we began to relax and enjoy the song. We listened to the strange melody long into the night, as the owls hunted along the edge of the swamp and in the nearby field. The moon rose in the sky, making the whole scene almost magical; the eerie song coupled with the silhouettes of the owls flying against the sky sent shivers up our spines.

The owls would disappear into the swamp, then return to the cavity of the tree. We supposed that they had young, because of the frequency of the trips, but we would not dare disturb the nest no matter how badly we wanted to see the owlets.

We followed the owls about the landscape, marveling at the variety of their diet. They would just as easily eat insects as they would voles and mice, and we were really surprised when we saw one take a green frog from the edge of the swamp. For the remainder of the nesting season, we followed the progress of the owls until well after the emergence and rearing of the owlets.

Screech owls can be found in almost every country setting, and I have at times seen them around more suburbanized areas, especially near old fruit groves, which they seem to favor. In a town just north of where I grew up in New Jersey and near a building where my father ran a small business, I once watched a pair of screech owls raise their young. The nest was located only a few feet above the ground in a small birdhouse that I had put up a few years before. To look at the owls and the size of the birdhouse hole, I never expected that they could fit inside, but they did easily. They would forage the abandoned lots out behind the building or the water's edge about 100 yards away. They established habits in reaction to the flow of nearby human activity and so were not seen. Indeed, I would never have noticed them if it hadn't been for a band of scolding jays that gave away their position one evening.

Because of the way the birdhouse was built, I could occasionally remove the roof and study the owlets. One evening when I was on a ladder looking through the roof, the owls returned earlier than I'd expected. One called the other with unusually shrill tones and immediately both began diving at me. Their attacks were fierce and I retreated quickly. The next night I noticed a big tomcat on the ladder that I had carelessly left in place after the attack. The cat was pawing the birdhouse when the parent owls showed up. Again they immediately began their attack. I was worried that the cat was too big for them to handle, but one owl dove close, hit the cat across the head with its talon and knocked the cat off the ladder. As the cat ran by I noticed a huge bloody gash, and I had no doubt that the owls could do the same to me. Try as I might during the passing weeks, I could not befriend the owls nor even come close.

The average screech owl is about ten inches long, with a tail just over three inches and a wingspan of about twenty-three inches. They have streaked a plumage of gray and reddish feathers, and sport ear tufts that make these small owls look much like miniature great horned owls. Their fluffy feathers make them appear much larger than they really are and also enables them to be silent flyers. Their eyes are large, yellow, and round. They nest in hollow trees—sometimes even bird boxes—where they lay four to seven eggs, with incubation by both sexes for about twenty-three days. The list of animals these owls will eat is enormously extensive, but their food consists mainly of mice, insects, birds, lizards, spiders, frogs, salamanders, and even crayfish.

Eastern cottontail (*Sylvilagus floridanus*)

The cottontail is a frequent visitor to the country areas as well as many of the lawns of suburbia. It is a secretive, well-camouflaged little rabbit. It will often lie in hiding just a few feet from a prowling dog or fox, and though its scent can give it away, if the cottontail is downwind it will go unnoticed. It isn't as fast as other rabbits and hares, but it has the ability to run erratically through heavy brush where most predators cannot follow. It is constantly aware of its surroundings and the coming and going of most animals and has the ability to freeze its motion to escape detection. Upon approaching it, you will note the utter stillness of the animal, until you get too close and it zigzags quickly away.

Grandfather taught Rick and I to study this ability of the cottontail to freeze, blend in with the brush and shadow, and remain constantly aware of everything around. We spent many years studying the habits of the cottontail, watching it move through the landscape, freezing, sensing, then moving again, as it stopped repeatedly to check for danger, apparent or not. Because of this vigilance, the cottontail is quite difficult to stalk close and it baffles me that so many end up as dinner for predators.

Cottontail

The cottontail is one of the first small animals we began to track after becoming proficient at tracking deer. Though cottontails are quite difficult to follow, reading their signs from feeding areas, beds, runs, and trails is relatively easy. They don't need large foraging areas and thus wear in rather pronounced roadways throughout their home areas. We learned quickly that the cottontails are indicator animals, meaning that an area that can support a good cottontail population will also be host to many other animals, herbivores as well as a good assortment of carnivores. We learned quickly to not hunt or trap an area if it didn't have a healthy population of rabbits.

Outsmarting a cottontail is quite easy despite their uncanny ability to avoid danger. We would spot a rabbit at dusk, mark the location, and come back the next night to see if it returned to the same area at the same time. When it did we went there the next day and found a place to hide close enough to allow us to observe, and sometimes even touch, the animal.

Most people assume that the cottontail is helpless in defending itself, but that is far from the truth. One time, I grabbed one by the back of the neck to see what it would do. It let loose a loud scream and scratched me badly across the cheek with its back paw. Another time, as I lay with my face right next to a rabbit trail, a feeding rabbit lunged at me with its front paws and cut up my nose and chin. From that, I got a violent infection that cut a weekend stay in the woods down to one day. Essentially there is no animal in the woods that is helpless. Even a deer will kick violently, and bucks during the rut, or mating period, have been known to attack and kill a man, though this is rare.

The cottontail rabbit grows to about sixteen inches long, with a two-inch tail and ears about three inches tall. They are a grayish brown above, gray on top of tail, and white beneath. They can breed several times a year, providing the climate is warm enough and food plentiful; gestation is approximately thirty days, and litters usually include four to six young. The nests are oval in shape, lined with the belly hair of the mother and are usually snuggled securely into heavy brush. Young are weaned in about two weeks. The life span of a cottontail can reach up to eight years but due to predation and disease, that longevity is rare. These rabbits eat many types of vegetation, including tree bark and twigs. Often you will find the soft cottontail hair in their home areas, especially in the late spring and early fall when they shed.

Black-and-white warbler (*Mniotilta varia*)

The black-and-white warbler is one of my favorite warblers. It can climb effortlessly around the trunks of trees and is a treat to watch. They seem to hold on so easily, hardly ever missing a step or slipping, as if they have glue or suction cups on the ends of their toes. They are exact in every movement and, unlike the squirrels, almost never break off a chip of bark because of carelessness. They can cling upside down or hang under a limb with just as much ease as they climb the trunks. Even more amazing is their systematic foraging of the tree trunks for insects. Hardly a nook or cranny goes unnoticed or untouched, which is often helpful to the trees, since the warblers pick away many of the damaging insects that would eventually harm the tree.

I once found a tree on which some black-and-white warblers had been feeding and I checked thoroughly about two square feet of bark that they had not yet searched. Even with a hand lens I could see no insects, insect eggs, or anything else the warblers might consider edible. Eventually the warblers came back and in no time at all were searching the area I had just scrutinized. To my amazement they quickly found several insects and mites, then upon searching again they found several more. They have been tremendous teachers by showing us how to search an area carefully, piece by piece, patiently, and effectively. They are so efficient it's as if they were commissioned by the tree for a thorough cleanup. A warbler's ability to go exactly to the place on a tree that has the most insects, even though they may not have been at that tree before, is uncanny. They are true insect trackers, and I have a lot of respect for anything that can track insects over bark.

To track the warbler up the bark of trees can prove extremely difficult. Unlike squirrels, rodents, and birds that are quite easy to spot and track, the warbler seems almost to float up the tree bark rather than touch it. The marks are at best very slight and even if you do find a single scratch, it is still difficult to find the entire track. We spent hours scrutinizing the barks of trees we had seen warblers climb and although we never found more than a few trace tracks, our ability to find larger animal tracks on bark increased dramatically.

The first time I found a warbler nest, I was amazed at how exposed and vulnerable it was. Although it was well camouflaged, it was merely a depression on the ground at the base of a shrub and was lined only with a few soft grasses and leaves. (Nests found in the following years were oftentimes not lined at all.) I watched the nest for the entire brood season, from the appearance of eggs to when the young warblers fledged. What I discovered was the young warblers' fine ability to lay perfectly still and quiet until the parent came, thus protecting themselves from wandering predators.

The black-and-white warbler is about four to five inches long, with a two-inch tail and a nine-inch wingspan; the female is smaller than the male. Both sexes are covered with black and white stripes, which helps them blend easily with the mottled bark pattern of many trees. Nests are built in the soft leaves at the base of trees or shrubs and sometimes lined with soft plant materials. Four or five young are born after a fourteen-day incubation period. Warblers eat most insects found in trees and bark, such as scaled insects, plant lice, caterpillars and various moths and beetles.

Boat-tailed grackle (*Quiscalus major*)

To many people, the nest-building antics of this large and beautiful member of the blackbird family is a sure sign of spring. Early in the season flocks begin to stake out territory and nesting sites in large trees, the stronger grackles usually getting the best spots. This activity is accompanied by continuous chatter and loud calling that lasts from dawn to dusk. It's funny to watch the habits of the flock. A most apparent paradox is how they argue so in the roosting and nesting trees, yet when on the ground feeding, they seem to tolerate each other. Many times after I have seen a nasty argument between two grackles in a tree, I've seen them fly to the water's edge and feed quietly side by side.

The grackle was the first bird I ever touched, though it was quite by accident. I'd been sitting quietly in a tree watching a nearby pond, when a grackle landed on a twig beside me. It paid no attention to me but busied itself arguing with another grackle perched on a lower limb. I reached out and touched it on the tail but it didn't move. I then touched it on the back of the head, and this time it turned slightly and took a halfhearted peck at me. When it realized that my hand was not another grackle, it screamed in fright and flew off. Of all the birds I've touched, I've probably touched more grackles than any other type.

Climbing into a tree to view a grackle can be quite hazardous—not so much because the grackles will attack but because the nests are usually out on limbs that look as if they can hardly support the weight of the nests. I go into the grackle trees just before dawn, well camouflaged, and climb very slowly and carefully, nestling close to the trunk. I am always afraid of scaring off the nesting grackles permanently, so I use the utmost caution. Mankind interferes with grackles too much as it is. I also never try to approach too close to a nest but rather sit near and watch the nesting process. After several visits, if you have made no move to endanger them, the grackles will get used to your presence and go back to their normal habits.

Since grackles live in flocks, there will be several nests in a tree, and you can find other birds nesting there also, especially in the smaller, outer branches where the grackle nests would be too heavy. I love to lie near a grackle tree in the early morning and listen to the wealth of birdsong and calls that come from the tree. Even in early spring when the grackles are just beginning to carry on and the greenery is beginning its upward swing, you can shut your eyes and envision the warmer times to come. There is no way one can get bored watching the nesting grackle, for there is so much to see, so many calls to learn, and so many habits to understand, including the interactions among grackles.

One of the most fascinating things to watch is the actual building of the nests. With utmost care the grackle will place twigs in an interlocking circle, larger twigs on the outside for support, smaller ones plus vines toward the center for density, and will cement the entire structure with mud. These nests are heavy and quite durable and will often visibly weigh down the branches in which they rest. Unfortunately, many of the nests built in the outer limbs *will* fall during heavy storms, which is probably one of the reasons for the grackles' arguments over nest position in the first place.

The male grackle can grow to about seventeen inches long and the female to about fourteen inches. Next to the closely related great-tailed grackle, the boat-tailed grackle is the largest member of the blackbird family. The overall coloring of the male is black, but when the light is right, you can detect a purplish sheen on the tail, head, and rump, and a greenish or bluish cast over the rest of the body. At times the bird appears to be metallic. Females tend to be a blackish brown with an underlying hint of smoky gray. The tail is as long as the body and flows out behind the bird like the straight keel of a boat. The eyes are yellow in the male, and a dark brown in the female. The nests are built in trees, usually far out on the limbs, and sometimes in shrubs, but always near some source of water. Nests are cup-shaped, built of twigs and other plants and held together with mud. The female takes care of the young. Insects make up the principal diet, especially beetles and grasshoppers, but they will sometimes eat frogs, toads, small animals, crayfish, and lizards. Grackles found in beach areas will feed on shrimp and crabs.

Sparrow hawk (*Falco sparverius*)

The sparrow hawk is a fascinating little hawk, frequently seen along even the busiest roadways, backyards, and farmlands. They hunt the grasslands, especially where the vegetation has been allowed to grow unchecked for long periods. In your travels by car you can see them perched on telephone wires or hovering several feet over any strip of wild grass. They are beautiful, very quick on the dive, and have a seemingly boundless supply of energy. Their eyesight, as with all hawks, is keen, and they can easily spot the prey from afar and kill with deadly accuracy. I have rarely seen a sparrow hawk miss its mark.

I have found it almost impossible to get within close range of a sparrow hawk except near its nesting area. To approach a feeding area, I've always found it necessary to build an elaborate blind. Before I build a blind, I have to watch the hawks feeding and determine which is their favorite feeding areas. I then locate their lookout tree and carefully build my blind. After constructing it, I will abandon it for a few weeks until the hawk gets used to it, and then I use it to watch the feeding habits. I have also built blinds near nesting areas to watch the hawks in the rearing of their young.

I did once get a chance to touch a sparrow hawk, or rather it touched me. I was climbing a tree and a sparrow hawk flew out of a cavity, the edge of which I was using as a grip. It attacked me repeatedly while I quickly climbed down and continued until I was well out of the territory.

Sparrow Hawk

The term "chicken hawk" is a misnomer that has arisen, I assume, out of an undue fear people have of hawks. Certainly a large hawk would take a chicken, if the chicken was quite a distance from a farm and if the hawk was desperate for food, but such a scenario is rare. I've always thought that, with the huge numbers of mice and rats the hawks kill around farms, they are well worth a chicken or two.

Even as a child I understood the need for hawks. Indeed, the sparrow hawk was the source of one of my first environmental battles. I was walking a trail that wound past a farmer's field when I was startled by a shot. I looked up and saw a sparrow hawk dropping from flight, some feathers askew, others drifting; it was as if the bird had exploded in midair.

Fearing the gun, I stalked to the edge of the field only to find a boy older than myself taking aim at another sparrow hawk perched in a tree. Without thinking, I picked up a heavy oak stick and hurled it at the boy as hard as I could. The stick hit him hard on the side of his head, blood began to pour, the gun went off, and he fell to the ground. He got up holding his head, and I froze with fear because I knew who he was, and worst of all he was the upper-class bully. He shouted, "I'll get you, Brown," then ran toward his house. My father got a call from his dad, and they both came to my house. I told the kid's father why I had thrown the stick, but at that time there were few laws against killing hawks. I thought that I was going to be beaten up, sued, and grounded till I was at least forty. But surprisingly, the boy's father thanked me. He said that he would have done the same thing and that his son did not have permission to use any gun.

I spent several days afterward searching the area where the boy had killed the hawk and finally found a hole in a tree that could have been the nest. I climbed the tree, carefully reached inside and removed five dead baby hawks. It sickened me to know that so many hawks had died because of one person's inconsideration, ignorance, and target practice.

After a few rocky weeks of anger over the incident, including a couple of fistfights, a two-day suspension from school, and a week's grounding at home, the boy who shot the hawk and I became friends. I even took him to the tree where the rotting hawk babies were and showed him what he had done. The lesson seemed to hit home, and in the years that followed he became a staunch defender of nature.

My favorite sparrow hawk was an old one that had perched outside the window of my fourth-grade classroom. Initially, it was a source of great aggravation for my teacher, until I explained the virtues and beauty of the sparrow hawk. I was then less often reminded to stop staring out the window and soon had the whole class and the teacher watching it hunt. That hawk stayed around for years, but by the time I graduated from sixth grade a younger hawk had taken its place. At the time I would have preferred to think that the first hawk had just moved on, but I knew that it had died. It was hard for me then to accept what I interpreted as cruelty in nature, but I've since learned that nothing in nature is needless or cruel. Only mankind can be cruel, not the laws of creation.

The male sparrow hawk can grow to as much as ten inches in length, with a twenty-two-inch wingspread, and the female to twelve inches long, with about a twenty-four-inch wingspread. The crown of the hawk is an ashen-blue with a black patch on each side of the head, near the cheek. The back of the male is an apricot or is cinnamon color with black barring; the tail is a reddish-brown with thin black bars and the wings grayish. The female is darker in coloration. Nests are built in hollow trees, hills, rock cavities, and bank burrows. Both sexes incubate the eggs for thirty days. The young remain in the nest for about three weeks and will obtain plumage after a year and a half. Hawks usually mate for life. They feed primarily on mice and insects, though they are known to hunt small birds, rabbits and other small animals.

Muskrat (*Ondatra zibethica*)

My most memorable encounter with the muskrat was my first. I had seen their tracks along a streambank and was determined to see the muskrats themselves. I had just turned eight years old and had an insatiable appetite for nature. Anything I saw intrigued me. It was winter and very cold but my determination pushed me out long before dawn to the blind I had built. I was going to see a muskrat no matter how early I had to get there. I sat for hours till I grew tired of waiting and was frozen to numbness. I was in the process of packing up my things when the first muskrat broke the surface of the water. I stood still and watched, so excited I felt as if my heart were going to leap from my chest.

Two smaller muskrats followed and stayed close to the first. They spent a long time by the riverbank, periodically diving and resurfacing. The cold water didn't bother them at all. To them it might as well have been an August afternoon. Finally, they carried some vegetation out of the muck and began to float back to their house. I hadn't noticed the house before, because the domed shelter had blended in with the old cattail so easily. I explored the perimeter of the house for quite some time before starting home. It was then that I realized I was no longer cold and I was mildly sweaty. I was surprised at what a little excitement could accomplish.

That muskrat house became a source of exploration for an

entire summer. Rick and I spent many hours around the dome, watching the muskrats and their new family. We would camouflage our heads with water plants and swim near them. At other times, covered with mud, we would wait by their holes and with caution touch them as they slipped out. We always took pains not to get *too* close or make our presence too apparent. There was the possibility of getting bitten—muskrats have very sharp teeth and I was once bitten by a young muskrat while trying to free it from someone's homemade trap. More importantly, however, we didn't want to frighten them into abandoning their snug little home. Years later, the muskrats were killed off by the river's pollution.

One of my favorite areas is the estuary system of Barnegat Bay in New Jersey. When we were young, Rick and I would build a raft from dead vegetation, driftwood, and mud, then camp on it for days on end. Usually the local muskrat population would become accustomed to our presence and begin to use the platform as a feeding area. They would climb on top and munch on a juicy tidbit only a few feet from where we were working. Sometimes they would approach closer, especially if we laid down a succulent water plant that they liked. After a long stay on the raft we would have all the muskrats named and were able to identify them by various markings, scars, and even personalities. It was the muskrats that first taught us that no two animals were alike no matter how similar they appeared. There is always a personality difference.

I will always remember one particular muskrat, which was probably the last descendant of those first muskrats I encountered. After a long absence, Rick and I had come back to the original muskrat house and found it dilapidated and caving in. After searching for fresh muskrat signs, we decided that they all must have died. (Also, during the previous year we had found several dead muskrats along the riverbank.) With care we removed the top layers of the house and laid the material nearby, so we could put it back together if we found any fresh muskrat signs inside. As we looked around the upper chamber with a flashlight, we found what we thought to be a small newly dead muskrat against the chamber wall. When we removed it to determine the cause of death, it awoke and tried to jump off my hand. The movement, however, produced hardly a frail stagger and the little muskrat lay back down. We didn't think that the muskrat was going to live, but we took it home in the hopes that we could nurse it back to health.

The first week was difficult as we tried many different food plants that we had seen the muskrats eating. Finally, out of desperation, we cut a few succulent shoots of cattail and force-fed it and forced water down its mouth. One evening the muskrat appeared to be dying and we were sure that it was not going to make it through the night. We went to sleep believing that we had done all we could and that we would have to bury it in the morning.

Morning came and I found the muskrat sitting upright in its box and munching some succulents near its pan of water. During the next week the muskrat grew stronger and fatter, each day looking less and less like the muskrat we had removed from its shelter. After a month it was happy and frisky, loved being held and petted, and romped unattended around the yard for hours. Each night, no matter how far it would wander, or how close to the stream, it would come back to the box. We were relieved that it was feeding on its own but we didn't like the fact that it was so friendly toward us. We decided to handle it less.

Still it persisted in coming to us and we feared that this unnatural kinship with humans could leave it defenseless when it went back to the wild. Our fears were dissipated some when a friend walked into my yard one day and the muskrat ran from him. We decided that though the muskrat was small, we would release it into the wild before it befriended anyone else. The following week we took it to an island in the estuary where we knew it would be with its own kind and relatively safe. When released it plunged right into the water, but it returned a few hours later to sleep on our platform. This continued for the days we stayed. The day we left we looked back only to see it standing on the platform again.

Each evening we came back to find it on the platform. Apparently we would have to help it build a home. The following week, as best as we knew how, we tried to duplicate the nest we had pulled it from, using mud and weeds to construct a dome right on top of the island. Finally we built a tunnel—to gave it a water exit—put the muskrat inside and capped the structure. A little while later it emerged from the tunnel and climbed atop the platform, but later that afternoon it retired back to the shelter and slept. Our work finished, we reluctantly slipped away in the evening. I don't know if the muskrat survived that season, but to this day the shelter is there, rebuilt a number of times and always occupied by muskrats. I like to think they are descendants of the original dweller.

Muskrats can grow to twenty-five inches, with a ten-inch tail. Their tail is flattened on the side, has little hair, and is covered with scales. Their shape is rather round, they have deep brown fur and dark gray underparts. Their ears are short and round, hardly breaking the hairline. They love waterways and especially marshes, where they dig bank tunnels or build mounds from mud and vegetation. Up to eight young are born about a month after breeding, and in relatively undisturbed areas where the food and water is plentiful, there may be up to three litters a year. The mother is the principal caregiver. Though their food is mainly aquatic plants, and some terrestrial plants, they will eat shellfish and other small aquatic animals. Houses usually have an under-water entrance that leads to the inner chamber high above the waterline.

Porcupine (*Erethizon dorsatum*)

Unfortunately, I did not get to see a porcupine till I was in my teens. In our area there were just no porcupines, so I was thrilled when my parents decided to take us on a weekend trip to the Adirondack mountains in upstate New York. I knew that there would be a few animals there, like bear and porcupine, that I couldn't find in the Pine Barrens in New Jersey. I read everything I could find about the animals in the Adirondacks, and I knew that it was prime area for porcupine. After camp was set up, I scouted the area and to my delight found a large assortment of porcupine tracks, chews, scat, and even three dropped spires, or quills, along one of the trails. The night sky overtook me, and I was forced to abandon my efforts until early the next morning. Because my excitement precluded any real sleep, I was well awake and ready to go before first light.

I wandered the landscape, following partial "porky" trails, hoping to find one ending at a tree, their usual nesting place. By afternoon I was exhausted and afraid I would once again run out of time. I decided to rest a bit under a grand pine tree. After I had eaten, I lay back against the tree and watched the sky. Suddenly I heard a distinctive munching and there directly above me was a *huge* porcupine. I was so excited that I forgot all danger and climbed the tree, almost falling when a dead branch collapsed. The near fall quieted me and I was able to ascend the tree to a good lookout area. There, not ten feet in front of me, sat my first porky.

I was rewarded even further when it began to move out to the end of an adjacent branch. What I had thought was a part of its tail was really a young porcupine, less than a quarter the size of the mother. It followed the mother closely, as if afraid to be on its own. It did climb easily and seemed to have no trouble with balance. I watched them till I could no longer see them because of darkness. On the way down I got a painful reminder of the porcupine, impaling my arm on a quill that had been wedged sideways in some loose bark. It took quite some time to dig it out, since pulling only set the barblike head in wider.

Many years later, I had another experience with the porcupine that wasn't quite as pleasant as the first. I was on a solo canoe trip in Canada. A good distance from any civilization, I was camped along the river and quite exhausted from a full day of paddling. In order to catch a ride back home, I had to make it back to a little hamlet on the water's edge by the afternoon of the next day. I thought I could easily make the trip back the next day with a few hours to spare. That night I was continually awakened by grinding of some sort, but I was too tired to check and figured it was just the water lapping along the banks. I awoke the next day to find the handle of my canoe paddle chewed off and the midsection chewed through. A porcupine had done it, because of its insatiable thirst for salt. The salt from my sweaty palms had saturated the ash wood of the paddle at the handle and midsection. Luckily I made it back, with not a moment to spare, but I'd wasted hours making a new shaft for the paddle and had blisters for weeks after due to the rough wood.

Another bad experience with porcupines occurred when they ate through a platform I had built to observe a nearby swamp. When I fell asleep on the platform that night, the chewed end gave way and I fell several feet to the ground, unhurt but angry. I couldn't really blame the porcupine, since it was following its instincts, and after all, I was the trespasser. The porcupine has certainly taught me patience and tolerance, and not a month after my platform broke, I had a grand experience that put the porcupine back in my good graces.

I had built another platform, nearby to the first one, but this time I checked it every day for porky signs. One night I saw a shape enter a cavity of a tree a few feet from my stand. The moonlight was strong enough for me to see that it was a porcupine and that it was taking great care in selecting a hole. Early the next morning before the sun broke the horizon, I peered into the elongated cavity. There in the dawn's first light I saw the mother give birth. The baby looked like a wet, tiny version of the mother, and by noon it was walking around. I figured that I was going to have several days watching this little one grow, but by the evening of the second day it followed its mother right up the tree. It was a little shaky and slow but it still followed. I was thoroughly amazed at its ability such a short time after birth. Later I saw it way up in the branches nursing, and the next day they were gone from the tree completely. I did see them again about three months later (I recognized the slit in the mother's ear) and the young one was still nursing. It seems something of a paradox that an animal that can climb a tree the second day after birth still has to nurse more than three months later.

The defense system of the porky is well known and very effective. From some distance away, I once watched a dog toying with a porcupine. I tried to yell at the dog to back it off, but it was too interested in its quarry. A dog that has encountered the tenacious quills will avoid a porcupine from that moment on. This dog barked repeatedly and charged, always falling short of biting the

porky. The porcupine showed no real fear but ambled toward a
rock outcropping and to the safety of a hole. The dog, seeing that
the porky was headed for cover, lunged at the animal and tried to
bite its back end. The dog let out a wail and rolled backward,
desperately trying to dislodge the quills by wiping its face along
the ground. The dog's master and I spent the remainder of the
day pulling about twenty-five quills from the dog's nose, tongue,
and muzzle.

Porcupines can grow up to about thirty inches long, have a
seven-inch tail, and will weigh between twenty and sixty pounds—
the average being about thirty pounds. Males are usually larger
than females. They are brownish black in color, with the quills
sporting a white base and black tips. The tail can be swung in
defense if a pursuer gets too close. The teeth of porcupines are a
bright orange and can be seen from quite a distance. They prefer
deeply wooded areas, especially coniferous forests, and they will
den in the cavity of a tree or rock outcroppings. They breed in
the fall, giving birth to a single young in the spring. The young
can walk within several hours of birth, climb within two or three
days, but will nurse for four months. They prefer evergreen foliage
and bark but will eat some water plants and the inner bark of
other trees.

Red-tailed hawk (*Buteo jamaicensis*)

The red-tailed hawk, because of its size, its splendid flight, and its
powerful diving, is probably my favorite hawk. Each time I see
one of these hawks circling a field or woodland area I am spell-
bound. Over and above its physical grandeur, what draws me
most is this hawk's inherent spirituality. Grandfather said it was
one of the birds closest to the Creator. I have come to know the
hawk as a spiritual entity, honoring it anytime it is sighted. It is a
symbol of freedom, of "good medicine," and of the Great Spirit,
and embodies the Native American attitude of "living with the
earth."

Rick and I once spotted a huge hawk, atop an old pine tree,
standing on the outer edge of her nest feeding her fuzzy

"hawklettes." We ran to get Grandfather, animatedly telling him what we had found. We knew that it was a hawk, but we were too young and inexperienced to know what kind. The three of us sat for hours at the perimeter of the area being careful not to show ourselves or alarm the hawk in any way. It was absolutely magnificent to watch the parent hawks hunt the nearby fields. They rarely missed their prey and killed them so quickly that I never heard a scream or squeak. They would dive, disappear into the grasses, then lift off carrying a limp animal in their talons. Small animals like mice were lifted with only one talon, while larger game needed both feet and made their flying look cumbersome.

We watched the hawk family through the entire brooding season, coming by every other day to check the progress of the young. I became so interested in the hawks that I took books from the library and had my parents read them to me. I was too young yet to read or understand the advanced books, so my parents helped. The hawk was the first animal I studied with such fervor, and that fervor became the stepping stone and example for the way I would study all other animals. I could easily watch those hawks for an entire day and frequently did. I never became bored, for each day the young ones grew and exhibited new behavior, and the adults were always doing something I had not seen before.

The ability of the hawk to see for long distances became obvious to me even after only a day of observation. I would watch as they soared high into the sky, almost out of sight, then in a flash streak to earth and hit their mark. Many times their prey was a mouse or some other small rodent, and I could not believe that they could see such small animals from such a great distance. I couldn't even see the mice through binoculars at a comparable distance. I know that with eyesight that keen they could easily see us at the edge of their clearing or hiding at the field's edge, but they paid no attention to us. I guess that they must have known we were not any threat to them, their young, or their prey.

I inadvertently helped the parents one day as I walked across the far area of their hunting field. When I got midway across, I noticed that they both dove from a tree next to the nest and hit the grasses about twenty yards beside me. They both rose with the small rabbits I had flushed out. One dropped a tail feather as it departed, and Grandfather said that it was a gift in return for helping them. I cherish that feather as good medicine and have it to this day.

The red-tailed hawk has been a source of inspiration and a great teacher. The most valuable lesson I have learned from the hawk is one I use in my classes to teach the value of other people's opinions. Rick and I were lying at the edge of a field waiting for a big cottontail to begin its late-day feeding cycle. It appeared suddenly from a feeder trail not far from us and began to feed not ten feet away. Its size was spectacular, probably exceeding the normal rabbit weight by about a pound. By looking at it, I could tell that it had been around for quite some time. Like a flash, a hawk hit the rabbit, killing it almost instantly. We were so close to the kill site that Rick was splattered with blood.

Being that close to a hawk killing was to me a once in a lifetime occurrence, but instead of reveling in what we both had experienced, we began to argue. Rick said that the hawk had first hit the rabbit with only one talon, then brought the other up and finished the job. I said that it had definitely hit with both talons right behind the head and killed the rabbit instantly. The argument became so vicious that we were headed to a fight. We didn't know that Stalking Wolf had watched the whole thing from the other end of the field and was on his way toward us. When we saw him, he told us both to keep quiet, because he wanted to teach us a valuable lesson—the same lesson the hawk wanted us to learn.

Grandfather placed a deer skull between us and asked me what I saw. I said I saw a deer skull—the nose, the teeth, and so on. He then asked Rick what he saw, and Rick said he saw the back of the skull, the place where the spinal cord attached to the skull, a fracture and hole in the backside of the skull where it had been struck, some mouse chews, and so on. Grandfather then asked me if I could see the hole in the skull and I said no. He then asked Rick if he could see the teeth or the nasal cavity, and Rick responded no. He then asked us both what we were looking at and together we said, "A deer skull," and we wanted to know why he'd asked. He simply said, "You both look at the deer skull but see it from different angles, from your own unique position. Is that not the way with all people in all situations?"

That incident became known as the lesson of the hawk and rabbit. Essentially, what Grandfather was saying was that no two people see the same thing, even if they are watching something at the same time. By virtue of each person's position, prejudice, upbringing, history, and uniqueness, everyone will see things very differently from others. It is rare that two people will see or even feel exactly the same way about anything. We must accept that uniqueness in people and listen to their teachings. They can do something we can't; they see something through different eyes and a different soul. Thus each person at once is a teacher and a student. Later on in life, after I began to read the works of Ralph Waldo Emerson, I was shocked to find how close in attitude Grandfather and Emerson were.

Every time I see a hawk I think of that hawk and rabbit lesson and the so many others that hawks have taught me. Once the lesson was simply a sign. It was at the time I was first trying to decide whether or not to write a book. I did not want to tie myself down to anything; I wanted to escape to the woods with my new family and take care of myself. When a publisher asked me if I would write a book, I left it up to the Creator. In prayer I asked for a definite sign that the book was the right way to go. I walked out of the house and there above me circled four hawks, calling to each other. At that time my home was in a development and I hadn't seen a hawk in the six months I'd lived there. One circled down and settled on the upper branches of the large English elm that grew in the front yard. There was no doubting that sign.

Red-tailed hawks are found not only in the countryside but also along any roadway that passes through the country or outer suburban areas. The abandoned fields and grass strips found along any major highway make good feeding areas. If you look carefully, you can see the hawks sitting in branches, usually the branches that afford the best views of their hunting fields. They seem oblivious to traffic, and one can approach them by stalking up from behind to where they are roosting. The noise and movement of the traffic usually helps camouflage your approach. Take care, however, whenever approaching a hawk, especially a nesting hawk, as they can attack viciously and cause serious wounds.

Red-tailed hawks grow to about two feet long and have very broad wings measuring to fifty-five inches across. The tail of the adult red-tail is—as its name states—red. Its overall color is grayish-brown above, with lighter wings and a white belly, and has a brown band running across the lower belly. The male is smaller than the female by a few inches. They mate in late winter and usually pair for life. Their nests are built in tall trees and made of loose sticks that look thrown together rather than woven. Incubation of eggs lasts about twenty-eight days. They feed on all manner of mammals, and will sometimes eat insects and snakes when other food is scarce.

Great horned owl (*Bubo virginianus*)

The great horned owl has always been shrouded in mystery and lore. The result, unfortunately, is much senseless killing and great misunderstanding. The fact that an owl leads a silent, nocturnal existence does little to dispel the mystery, and the call of the owl at night and its muffled, sometimes silent, mothlike flight sends chills up campers' spines. An owl is rarely seen by day, but it is possible if one knows what signs to look for and what kind of tree the owl prefers during the day. Owls are enormously adept at camouflage and can, at a glance, look like part of the tree trunk or a broken-limb stump. An owl is sometimes spotted by people when a crow or a jay dives on it and scolds.

Grandfather took great pains to teach Rick and me the habits of the owls and how to locate the owls in the day and night. They were great lessons that also helped us to understand the habits of a great many other nocturnal creatures. My first lesson from the owl taught me the profound interconnectedness of nature. We were following Grandfather down a trail by our medicine cabin in the Pine Barrens. We always watched him closely, duplicating every move he made, looking every place he looked, fearing that we might miss something. Many times, when we weren't paying attention, he would point out something grand, something obvious if only we had been paying close attention to him or the landscape.

On this particular day he kept his eyes to the ground, never looking up as far as we could tell. As we passed under a branch of a rather thick pine tree, he turned to us suddenly and said simply, "Don't disturb him." We looked at each other with chagrin; obviously we had missed something. We carefully examined the ground and found nothing. In wild desperation we searched the outer landscape and closer brush—still nothing. Finally, after a long time, we gave up. Rick sighed and looked toward the sky in disgust. There, only a few feet above us, hidden by the needles of the pine, roosted a huge great horned owl. We were absolutely flabbergasted, amazed at being so close to such an elusive creature. What puzzled us most was how Grandfather knew, without looking up, that the owl was in the tree.

We ran to him, completely ignoring the owl, and asked him how he knew the owl was in the tree without even looking up. Grandfather, being a coyote teacher and thus never telling something that we could learn by experience, said, "Go ask the mice." We knew quite well what he meant. There was no way he could tell us or show us how he knew, because there were certain things he could not easily explain, but he did give us a clue: the mice! We studied the mice for many months till our knees became calloused and the top of our feet began to grow knots or bone spurs. Not only did we know what the mice did when owls were around but also, by studying mice we knew what mice did whenever anything else was about. From that encounter with the owl, we learned many lessons, including how everything was interconnected and how nothing could move in nature without disturbing something else.

Even today, whenever I see or hear an owl of any sort, it is always a treat. I especially love seeing them on moonlit nights when they flutter across the horizon like huge silent moths. The first time I witnessed an owl catching its prey was on a harvest moon night, when the moon appears so big and full. I was sitting at the edge of a small clearing, leaning against a tree and watching the moon rise. The stillness of the night was overwhelming; nothing seemed to be moving. I should have realized that such stillness was a sure sign that some predator was about. The clearing in front of me glowed with moonlight, and I could see everything clearly. An owl launched itself from a tree, flew toward me, then dropped to the low brush a few yards in front of me. In its talons it caught a vole and proceeded to swallow it head first. I realized that the vole had been taken from under the leaves and that the owl must have heard it since there was no way the owl could have seen it. I had read how acute the owl's hearing is, but up till than I hadn't understood what that meant.

The male owl can grow to about twenty-two inches long, has a tail just under nine inches, and a better than fifty-inch wing-spread. The females are larger and can grow to twenty-five inches with as much as a fifty-eight-inch wingspread. They have distinctive ear tufts, with color patterns resembling that of the screech owl, large yellow eyes, and loose oversize feathers that make the bird silent in flight. They nest in groves, caves, and heavy timber, sometimes taking over an abandoned crow or hawk nest to raise its young. Two to five eggs are incubated by both parents for up to thirty days. The young are snowy white. Their main food is rabbit, rats, and mice, but they will take insects, birds, and even fish. They have powerful claws and beaks and can catch and easily kill woodchucks, porcupines, skunks, and even geese and turkeys.

Barn owl (*Tyto alba*)

One of my greatest thrills when I was a child was exploring abandoned buildings and forgotten towns of the Pine Barrens. All manner of animals utilize these buildings for shelter or hunting grounds. It seems that whenever man abandons a building, nature is quick to take it over and heal the scars it made on the land. This takeover and eventual collapse of man's structures gives me hope that nature can and will prevail. In these abandoned buildings, towers, and barns the barn owl makes its home and raises its young.

Once I was searching an old barn with a flashlight when my light hit the face of a barn owl, though I didn't realize that was what it was. Its face moved up and down and from side to side, and scared me out of the building as fast as I could go. I told Rick what had happened and decided that it must have been a ghost that wanted me out of there. Grandfather came by shortly thereafter and wanted to show us something. We followed willingly until we came to the abandoned barn. I would not go in and told him the story of the ghost that lived in the rafters. He laughed heartily and told us that it was an owl he wanted to show us, not a spook. I went in, albeit reluctantly, and to my great delight—and relief—saw four barn owls sitting in a row on a lower beam.

Today, in my teaching, I use the barn owl when demonstrating nature awareness. Classes are held in an old barn, and after a few days of lectures I ask the students to point out the nearest owl. Usually no one has seen one, nor do they see one until they learn, through tracking, to look for the appropriate signs—in this case, owl pellets. Owl pellets are regurgitated bits of indigestible matter, such as bones, hair, and claws—to name just a few things. Where these pellets are found, an owl is usually roosting nearby or overhead. Fortunately, for the sake of my awareness lecture, there have always been owls in my barns, and I have used four barns in the last decade for lectures. Unfortunately, as old buildings are knocked down, fewer barn owls are finding suitable quarters for roosting nearby.

The male barn owl is usually fourteen to twenty-one inches long, with a tail of just seven inches and a wingspan of forty-seven inches. The female can grow to twenty-four inches long with a slightly longer tail and a forty-nine-inch wingspan. Except for the Northern Snowy owl, they are our lightest colored owls, with male and female, adult and young sporting a large, white, heart-shaped face. They nest in hollow trees, abandoned buildings, and sheltered crevasses. There is no actual nest built, and the eggs are laid right in the open, with no protection. Five to nine eggs are incubated by the female for about thirty-three days. In good conditions, in the more southern areas, the barn owl can have two broods a year. Their primary diet is mice and rats.

PART IV:
TRACKING AND STALKING IN THE FORGOTTEN WILDERNESS

TRACKING

Tracking is tracking whether it is done in the urban and suburban areas or in the wilderness, but there are some important points that should be kept in mind when tracking on either urban or suburban "terrain." For one thing, the "good" tracking areas in such places are limited, and often broken up by hardtop roadway or concrete. Areas such as parking lots, roadways, and sidewalks can be tracked but are best left to the more experienced, since it can take innumerable hours of "dirt time" before the tracker can accurately read the signs on hard ground and pavement. And so, although tracking is essentially the same—no matter where you are—there are some simple rules and guidelines that must be followed in the more urbanized areas. This section is intended as a short review of some of the tracking techniques outlined in my other field guides.

WHERE TO FIND TRACKS

It will become evident rather quickly that animals found in the urban and suburban setting cannot be followed very easily because of hard-topped areas that apparently obliterate any tracks. As I tell all my tracking students, however, the importance of a track is not that you follow an animal to the end of its trail but that you be able to read what any portion of trail is telling you. For instance, if I wanted to choose a place at a line of trees by my house to see deer pass, I would be at a loss if I didn't have the ability to read tracks. Since I would not be able to tell where the deer were coming through, my choice of location would be haphazard at best. But, if I can find a portion of trail and see that many deer have passed the area frequently, I can set my blind by that area. And, if I can read the age of the tracks, I can tell what time they pass and be there at that time instead of wasting an entire day waiting for them to show up. The same holds true in any urbanized area. Tracking will tell you what animals are in the area, what their routes of travel are, what time they pass, and much about their habits.

In any urbanized setting our attention should be drawn to the dirt areas, whether they be an abandoned lot, a window box, a garden, or even the collected dirt/dust strip skirting every roadway. The best areas are the muddy banks and soft ground surrounding water. These areas will yield the best tracks, those easiest to spot and follow for short distances. Patches of lawn are more difficult to track, but with a little practice you will soon be able to read the bent grasses and disturbed earth beneath.

Some of my students who live in the city build a tracking box to keep up on their tracking skills. A tracking box is simply a six-by-four-foot box, with six-inch sides, filled with play sand or soil that will hold tracks well. The soil is raked smooth, stamped and flattened lightly with a small board—the soil should be slightly damp to best hold any tracks—and bait is placed in the center. Peanut butter, bread, seeds, or even leftovers will make an enticing snack for any animals in the area. The box is then studied daily for tracks. Sometimes the sands literally turn into a fine tapestry of myriad tracks and patterns—a great way to learn when you can't get to the woods.

Whenever walking the sidewalks or the streets, you should become aware of all soft ground areas. I have found some grand tracks in the dirt squares around the bushes that grow in our cities. Look also at any tree, for the bark will hold very definite scratchings of many animals that climb and hunt for insects. The more you practice looking at the soft ground areas, the more aware you will become of tracks and the vast array of animals that exist right under your nose. Many times the track alone gives us a clue to where the animals will hide. True tracking does require patience, though; you might see an animal's tracks for months, or even years, before you actually see the animal for the first time. Focus your attention on all the soft areas, even window flower boxes, for this will bolster your awareness of the wildlife of your area.

HOW TO TELL TRACKS

There are two ways to tell what kind of animal has left a track. One is called **clear print classification**, referring to the identification of an animal from very clear tracks. The other method is called **pattern classification** and is used when instead of a clear track, you have a series of indistinct depressions linked together in a loose pattern. Both methods should be studied to the point that you can tell, in an instant, what animal has made the tracks. These methods are very easy to learn and anyone can begin to use them immediately.

  Clear print classification is a simple method of identifying mammal prints in which you can easily see the heel pad, all the toes, and even the claws. We will concern ourselves here with five specific families of animals—the ones most often tracked and of the greatest interest: the cats, dogs, rabbits, weasels, and rodents. Clear print classification is done by counting the number of toes on one front foot and one rear foot. I use this front-foot/back-foot method because the foot prints of animals are usually grouped in two, one front and one rear together, thus you do not have to hunt for the next set of tracks.
  All members of the *cat family* (which includes among others, the feral cat, the mountain lion, the lynx, and the bobcat) have four toes up front and four toes in the rear, and because cats usually retract their claws when walking, there are rarely claw marks visible in the tracks.
  All members of the *dog family*, such as the feral dog, wolf, fox, and coyote, have four toes up front and four in the rear with their claws showing.

The *rabbit family* also have four toes up front and four in the rear, but the rear feet are two to four times larger than the front.

Members of the *weasel family*, including weasels, skunks, badgers, wolverines, mink, otters, martens, and fishers have five toes up front and five in the rear. Not in the weasel family but also having five toes front and rear are raccoons, opossoms, and bears, which are very flat-footed, while the weasels tend to walk on the balls of their feet.

Rodents, including all mice, rats, squirrels, groundhogs, chipmunks, muskrats, beavers, and porcupines, to name a few, have, with a very few exceptions, four toes up front and five toes in the rear.

Pattern classification does not yield as specific information as clear print classification does concerning the species of the animal, but it will at least put the animal into a general family group. Because nature gives us rarely clear prints, especially in the urbanized areas, this is the kind of identification my trackers are dealing with ninety percent of the time. The following are four major pattern classifications that should be studied carefully. These, along with the identified stride of an animal (using a field guide for measurements), will quickly identify the animal being tracked.

Diagonal walkers. These animals typically walk with one front foot and the opposite back foot together at a time. When they pick up in speed, the pattern will change, but remember that animals will walk most of the time. Generally as the right front moves forward, so does the left rear, with slower gaits producing variations in the timing of the diagonal leg movement. The pattern is simple to learn and looks very much like the walking pattern of a man, which in loose terms is also a diagonal walker. Animals that fall into this category are the deer family, the dog family, and the cat family.

Bound walkers. Unlike the diagonal walkers, bound walkers will usually keep to this pattern whether moving fast or slow. The movement consists of pushing out with the front feet, which strike the ground together, side by side. The rear feet then push off and land directly behind the front feet, also side by side. Animals that fall into this category are most members of the weasel family, with the exception of a few that will be discussed later. The weasels move in an undulating fashion, up and down, not dissimilar to a sewing machine needle at work.

Gallop walkers. Like the bounders, these animals, fast or slow, will generally maintain their track pattern. They will push off with their rear feet, hit with their front feet, then bring the rear feet around and in front of the front feet, resulting in a track pattern that has the rear feet preceding the front feet. When the squirrel lands, its front feet are side by side, but when a rabbit or ground-dwelling rodent lands, its feet are at a diagonal to each other. Members of this group of animals are rabbits, hares, and most rodents. (Those rodents that do not fall into this category will be discussed below.)

This feet-together pattern holds somewhat true of the birds, also. Perching birds—birds that spend much of their lives in trees—will, like the squirrel, hop across the ground, feet side by side. Those birds that spend most of their time feeding on the ground will hit with their feet diagonally, producing a track in the typical human walking pattern.

Pacers. Like the diagonal walkers, pacers will change their pattern as they pick up in speed. They will move the same side of the body at the same time. In other words, when the right front paw is moving forward so is the right rear paw. Typically, they look more like they are lumbering across the ground rather than walking or bounding. Members of this group are the raccoons, opossums, bears, striped skunks, badgers, groundhogs, porcupines, and beavers.

It is good to keep in mind, especially in tracking, that there are no absolutes. All of the above animals, whether diagonal walkers, bounders, gallopers, or pacers, are capable of changing their walking patterns depending on mood and circumstance. Fortunately for the beginning tracker, however, these walking patterns hold true ninety-five percent of the time. With patience and careful observation of animals as they move, a new tracker will begin to pick out the major distinctions—and the variations—in locomotion, as well as understand why a variation is taking place. All that is needed is patience, keen observation, and "dirt time."

SIGNS

Besides the typical track, there are many other signs that will tell of an animal's presence, and a good tracker should be aware of them all. Keep in mind that an animal will always take the easiest route of travel, unless pursued, and that animals are creatures of habit. When a route of travel is generally safe, an animal will take it repeatedly, thus wearing in a "roadway," which trackers know as trails. Smaller, less used roadways are called "runs." Once these trails and runs are located, it is much easier to see animals. At first you may have to guess what time the animal usually passes, but the more you know about an animal's habits, the better you can estimate what time it will be out and using its roadway system.

Other signs to look for include rubs, hairs, feathers, scratchings, gnawings and chewings, and scat—they will all tell a tremendous amount about the animal, its habits, and probably its whereabouts.

A *rub* is a place where an animal repeatedly rubs itself, whether intentionally or unintentionally. An intentional rub would be a favorite pole where a cat or raccoon scratches its side or back; an unintentional rub would be a place or object against which an animal accidentally rubs itself as it passes by. These areas, depending on how often they are rubbed, can be very smooth or just lightly shined.

Near or on any of these rub areas you are likely to find another sign—*hair*. A good tracker can tell not only from what animal a particular hair came, but also from where on its body. I learned to tell the differences in hairs by pulling the hair from various parts of the body of road-killed animals, taping them into my notebook and labeling them. This way, after a period of many years and through many notebooks, I can now tell the hair or feather of any animal or bird and the exact area of the body from which it came.

Scratchings are another sign. Whenever an animal scampers over sidewalks or debris, or climbs trees or poles, it will leave an array of scratches. Squirrels have elaborate arboreal trail networks of scratched limbs and branches that they use on a daily basis. If you climb park trees and look along the branches, you will note a huge assortment of scratches.

Gnawings and *chews* are other telltale signs of the presence of animals. Not only will these be found on the food they have been eating but also on the bits of bone that they gnaw for the calcium. By noting the approximate size and spacing of the teeth, the amature tracker can come very close to guessing the correct size and species of the animal.

The *scat*, or fecal matter, of animals is a particularly good sign, for it can identify not only the animal, but also what it has been eating, thus leading the tracker to the food source.

This section on signs and tracks is a light treatment of what is a very involved and complicated subject, an art form and a science. It takes many hours and years of dirt time to become even an averagely competent tracker, but with these helpful hints on identification, a whole new world should open up even for the beginner. Only through the art and science of tracking do we learn what we would normally miss with the eyes. Indeed, tracks are sometimes the first evidence we have that an animal exists in our area, and once our attention is drawn to the animal's existence we can begin searching. By my way of thinking, seeing an animal is exhilarating, but seeing the track of an animal opens a world far beyond the senses and tells of things that we would never know about an animal, if we used only our eyes. Next time you see a raccoon, ask yourself whether it is male or female, exactly how much it weighs, whether its stomach is full, empty, or half full. Only tracking can tell you that. Add the actual sighting of an animal to what you've observed in the study of its tracks and you will know more about an animal than you could ever learn from a thousand books or teachers.

STALKING AND CAMOUFLAGE

Stalking and camouflage in the more urbanized areas are at times easier and at times more difficult than in the wilderness. One of the most difficult problems to overcome—and it is quite funny if you think about it—is that the simple act of stalking in the city or suburban environment is likely to arouse a certain amount of suspicion. Picture what the police or general public will think if they see a person slowly, almost imperceptibly, moving through the shadows and heavy brush of our park areas, or standing motionless in a darkened alcove. You might very well be deemed a criminal or a crazy and perhaps even be arrested. Unless you are walking, and that usually means at a good pace, people will often assume that you are up to no good.

One evening in New York City, after finishing a speaking engagement, I decided to take a walk just outside my hotel at the lower end of Central Park. As I walked, the sun began to set and the shadows grew long. Suddenly, I heard the distinct voice of a screech owl; the tone was unmistakably a communication with its mate. I knew instinctively that the owl was near the nesting tree hollow, so I began a slow stalk. Following the sound intently, I slipped through brush and shadow, walking slowly, careful of each footfall and my motion an imperceptible flow until I reached the tree. There, just a few yards from a thicket and several feet up in the tree, was the hole of the screech owl, with the owl perched very close.

Suddenly I was surrounded by police. As I backed away from

195

the tree, onlookers gawked as I tried feebly to explain what I was doing and that there were owls living in Central Park. Try as I might, I could not convince the police that I was simply stalking and not a criminal, and there was no way in the world they would believe that there were owls in Central Park. Quickly, an elderly, elegantly dressed and apparently influential gentleman stepped from the crowd. To my luck he was an avid birdwatcher who had a residence near the park, and to my amazement he had read all of my books. He told the police to back off, asked that I continue my stalk and followed me, without regard for his well-tailored tuxedo, carefully through the tight brush. For the next hour I led police and citizen alike to the owl tree, and there heard my followers' gasps of delight at seeing or hearing the owls. No one could believe that such an animal could exist outside the zoo, and we spent hours in lively conversation. I was truly lucky that I was not spending the night in some Manhattan jail, deemed some type of criminal or lunatic.

The stories of my urban stalking are many, and fortunately each time I've come through without an arrest. What amazes me most, though, is the number of police or citizens who have become fascinated by the wonders I was stalking. The closest I came to being jailed was along the New Jersey parkway. This superhighway runs through some of the most beautiful and varied areas of the state, and the land bordering it is a haven for an incredible variety of wildlife. Once, after a long week of total survival living in the Pine Barrens, my class was on its way back to our farm—a motley, dirt-ridden crew, reeking of campfire smoke and artistically adorned in the latest ripped and worn fashions, and of course lavished with all manner of dirt and mud. I had made the apparent mistake of stopping to photograph a small deer feeding along the parkway when a group of police, flashing lights, hands near their guns, and faces grim, surrounded us. We had broken one of the cardinal rules of the road: "No stopping or standing."

I suspect that we must have looked like a bunch of drug-runners, or worse. The tone of the police, as they watched our every move and searched our vehicles, was not easy or mocking but measured and very professional. The irony of it all is that I teach classes to police military personnel, and many other public

servants, and I am often called upon to track criminals for local
and state police, and the FBI. But these were all rookies and my
explanations were not believed. To add insult to injury I have also
had New Jersey's governor's son in my school and the governor
himself is a well-rounded conservationist in his own right. I tried
everything that day but it looked grim, and I was afraid that we
were on our way to jail, when at last a car pulled up, carrying in
it a few local police chiefs and some high-ranking state troopers,
who quickly dispatched the problem.

Over the years, most of my stalking has been done in wilderness areas but because I have an insatiable curiosity concerning
all natural areas, wilderness or otherwise, I have learned the
savvy of stalking our more urbanized areas. And I've certainly
learned many tricks of the road that have kept me out of trouble
and out of jail. One such trick, which can also be quite useful in a
stalk, is to bring along a birding book and a pair of binoculars or a
camera. That way folks tend to ignore you as just another artist or
naturalist. Other times I've pretended to read a newspaper or
book, all the while keeping my eye on what I was stalking, the
book serving only as a diversion or cover, though this can be
distracting. If I am caught without any of these props and confronted by the police or an irate home owner during a stalking
trespass, I have learned that the best defense is a good offense. I
simply get real upset and say that I have lost my dog and I just
saw it a short distance away. Then I ask them to please, *please*,
keep an eye out for it. (It is a good idea to provide a thorough
description of your imagined dog, and make it not a mutt, but
something exotic like a schipperke or similar.) Ironically the authorities' hearts go out to you and you are let go on your way. But
remember to call the name of the dog as you walk away—and not
"Rover!"

Stalking in the city and suburbs, however, is not as demanding
an art form as it is in the wilderness or deep country. There is
usually no need for camouflage since animals native to these areas
are used to seeing people all the time. (Camouflage might also
make life difficult if you are approached by the police; it can be
almost impossible to explain.) As in the wilderness, though, we
still follow the wisdom of the heron, which teaches us how to hold

our upper bodies, and of the cat or mountain lion, which teaches us how to touch softly with our feet. Stalking is always slow, flowing, and never jerky. You use the natural brush and shadows like the weasels, slipping through these areas quietly so as not to disturb any twig or bush, always keeping hidden, and allowing the light to dapple your body with a natural broken pattern to become undetectable to animals, and people. In recent years, my stalking is so well planned that I am not only watching for what I am trying to stalk but also for anyone who would be looking my way. It is sort of like being an ancient Apache scout, evading enemies while stalking your quarry. This way there is no confrontation. The best defense is not to be seen by anyone, and that includes muggers hiding in the dark. Many times I've stalked them only to have them run screaming from their hiding places.

As I've said, stalking in the more urbanized areas can be a little easier than in the wilderness. Animals in the wilderness are not used to people; people are known to them as the most fearsome predators. Thus they are always on the watch. The wilderness landscape does not lend itself easily to the stalker, for there are always forest litter—dried leaves, plants, vines, pebbles, etc. —and tangles of brush to contend with, and there is no constant background noise to muffle a mistake. On the other hand, the urban and suburban environments lend themselves beautifully to the stalker. Not only are the animals used to people being about, but also the landscape is much more civilized, thus an easier stalk. Plus there is always constant background noise to muffle any mistake the beginning stalker would make.

Stalking in cities and suburbs is performed essentially the same way as in a wilderness situation, with just a few variations as dictated by the different conditions. As in any area, the stalker should utilize cover and shadow whenever possible, never stepping into direct light unless there is no other way to the quarry, staying close to buildings, alcoves, garbage cans and piles, or hedgerows and even automobiles. The more broken up the stalker's outline is the less likely an animal is to spot him. When I go to the city—for speaking engagements or to see my publisher—I carry with me clothing of dark gray or brown plaid patterns; the darker grays I save for night stalking. For footwear, I prefer well-worn sneakers. Moccasins and other soft leather footwear have a tendency to wear out quickly on concrete and city streets.

To stalk anywhere, the body is held upright, with the hands and arms held close to the body. This alters the typical human silhouette that animals know so well, and the tight, upright position probably appears to them to represent a pole or a pile of garbage. All movements should be so slow and flowing as to be almost undetectable.

In the city, the feet are placed on the ground or pavement in a manner different from what I have taught in my more advanced stalking books. The method I suggest for the city is one that the Apache people used when crossing rock faces or stone-covered areas. With all the weight on the rear foot, edge the front foot forward and bring it to the ground slowly until the outside edge of the heel just touches the ground. Slowly roll your foot from the outside heel to the inside toe in a soft, compressing fashion, feeling to make sure that you are not stepping on anything. This compression step will muffle any sounds that might be given off by the foot on the sidewalk, driveway, or grass areas. Once the foot is firmly planted, then the full weight is eased onto it and the process continued. Your eyes should be kept on the animal at all times and your motion should be frozen anytime the animal looks your way.

GRANDFATHER AND THE FISHERMAN

The tragedy in life is not what men suffer, but what they miss.

Thomas Carlyle

I grew up walking a fine line between two worlds, the world of modern society and what is to me the more intimate, real world of Grandfather's wilderness. Many times this line has grown very thin and I have lost my balance; fortunately I have always fallen into the wilderness; it is here I choose to stay. The wilderness is my reality, my teacher, my parent. It is the temple of the Creator, made by the Creator, and it is where the greatest lessons of life can be learned. The natural laws are immediate and real; time is not artificial but eternal. The wilderness is an old world with old values, but those values are as alive and true today as they were when all the people of the earth lived in these sacred places. I don't think I will ever truly understand modern man and his world, for I am a child of the wilderness and walk a very different path than most. I have been raised and taught by two distinct societies and can objectively compare them. For me the choice will always be the pure and wild.

The story I call "Grandfather and the Fisherman" is the story of the differences between the natural world and the artificial world, or society. For me these differences are between a life of intensity and rapture and a life of mediocrity and desperation, between life and death.

Both Grandfather and the fisherman were teachers, each a grandfather of the society they represented. Grandfather Stalking Wolf and I lived together for more than a decade; grandfather fisherman and I spent only a few short hours together. Each taught me, not through words, but through actions, forever changing my life, clarifying questions that had gone unanswered for years. I had been protected by the purity of the wilderness and Earth Mother for years and did not fully realize the differences between the two worlds. The differences and chasms between the two are at once awesome and terrifying, sometimes impossible to breach or even to comprehend. They are two extremes with much to teach: lessons that go beyond all description; lessons I still learn from, each day of my life; and lessons that confirm my choice of the wilderness and vision, and make my path very clear—a true choice of reality over superficial existence.

I was seated quietly on a tangled upper bank of the stream Rick and I used for our daily swims. It was early morning and I had come to the bank to watch the sunrise, the intensity of night turning so elegantly to day. Time seemed endless, each small event of major significance, everything in perfect harmony, balanced—what Grandfather called Oneness. I caught a slight movement out of the corner of my eye and I saw Grandfather moving toward the water down one of the little trails that led from camp. Just looking at him, actually seeing him, was a thrill. He always moved with such secrecy, that for me it was a treat to even think I had caught him unawares. He never seemed to walk the trails but rather floated, as if he moved on an invisible carpet of air, never making a sound, his body still. To watch him was like watching a well-choreographed forest ballet set to the music of the stream, the symphony of birdsong and the gentle rustle of warm breezes.

What he did then utterly shocked me—no, stunned me—though it shouldn't have. As he neared the water, he paused for an instant in an attitude of worship, as if praying but also reveling in the beauty that surrounded him. He then knelt gently and I could see his hand touch and fondle the cool dampness of the earth. Slowly, as if approaching the holiest of holy temples, he slipped down the bank of the river. Kneeling again, he bent toward the water and gazed into it for a long time, glancing up and down the stream now and again, savoring the sunlight dancing on the rifts and the light mists hugging close to the cathedral of cedars downstream. He gently reached his hand out over the water and began to touch its surface, almost as if petting it. Then with the same gentle touch he slid his hands beneath the surface, and I could see his fingers running back and forth as if he were feeling fine silk. He lifted a palmful to the Creator in thanksgiving, then released it to splash back to the stream in a glorious array of rainbows and waterdrops. At that point he slowly entered the water for his morning bath, each step of the way feeling the water's essence. Gazing at his face, seeing his actions, I knew the true meaning of sensuality—no, of pure rapture.

I was mystified to see this ritual, for such a rapturous entry into the waters was beyond anything words could describe. Here was a man that had swum a thousand rivers, streams, ponds, and lakes, yet he entered this one as a temple. It then dawned on me, like rocks thundering in my soul, that his behavior was nothing new. He entered *all* waters as if they were temples, the same way each time, savoring every moment, but this time I had really seen it and understood. I realized also that he acted this way with everything; no matter how many times he might have seen, touched, heard, tasted, or smelled an object, he would still fondle it in this reverent, most sensual way. To him, all things were not the same, each was always new. It was not simply a matter of thought or principle, but of feeling and experience. He was a true child of the wilderness and everything, from a grain of sand to a huge old cedar, was always fresh and new. Everything was an adventure, charged with the most rapturous excitement.

The few moments I spent watching Grandfather at the river forever changed me, dramatically and profoundly.

I was fifteen years old when the scenario of Grandfather at the stream took place. Though I had lived with Grandfather for about eight years, I had never truly picked up on the way he traveled the temples of creation. From that moment on, I watched him even more carefully then I ever had before. Everything was a mystery to him; adventure and excitement abounded wherever he would wander. Most important, he was completely and always filled with utter sensuality and rapture about the things around him, and about life itself. I would follow him, watch him stand gazing at a robin, or a flower, or a leaf, or a sunset. He would pat or hug trees, clutch the earth to his breast and breathe deep the aroma of soil and loam. He was totally alive, totally in tune, totally one with the Creator's wilderness, and hence one with the Creator. His days were devoted to thanksgiving, to touching, to living, to rapture.

I was raised by Grandfather for a little more than ten years and watched him move daily through the temples of creation, surviving, observing, tracking, and living easily and fully. His days were full of peace, love, and boundless joy. Come to think of it, all people, no matter what they do or how they go about it, are at heart working for peace, love, and joy, nothing else. The problem with modern man is that he thinks that these things can be found in externals—bigger cars, mansions, fat bank accounts, fame, or fortune. But such goals inevitably fall far short of expectation. I've walked that fine line between both worlds and I know that the wilderness is the only place to truly get in touch with self and peace, love, and joy.

The modern world, what I call the other world, and its malaise were revealed to me quite by accident. Like the wisdom of Grandfather and the water, this teaching of the fisherman came quickly, intensely, and unexpectedly. What was clarified by Grandfather, the fisherman hammered home in a lesson I will never forget. It happened quite innocently as I sat on the beach awaiting, once again, the rising sun. It was a public beach and just a few yards down from me sat an old fisherman in his beach chair, his line in the water, and his eyes on his pole. The sun had broken the water when we began to talk.

The fisherman had been fishing this same beach for over thirty years. Since he had retired, he returned every week or so to catch the bluefish, his favorite. We spoke of fish, how the area had changed, his new fishing reel and tackle, the weather, and myriad other things, till the conversation finally trailed off and I slipped back to my sunrise and he to the flicking end of his pole.

As I sat there, I reached down into the cool sand and picked up a good handful, feeling its silky dampness run between my fingers. I studied the fine crystals in my palm, fingering them so that the rising sun would bedazzle them when rays hit at just the right angle, making gorgeous colors, shapes, and shadows. The old fisherman's attention must have been drawn to my intent stare, since he yelled over, "What you got there?" Startled, I simply said beach sand. Looking at me a little puzzled, he asked me what I was doing with beach sand, and I replied, rather matter of factly, "Studying it." "Beach sand," he said. "It's just gray and white, with a few black flecky things in it." I was shocked to a point of speechlessness. I just couldn't comprehend that a man who had fished these beaches for over thirty years did not know what beach sand looked like!

I said, "Old man, please grab a handful of sand and have a look. Do yourself a favor." A little taken aback by the tone and command in my voice, he immediately reached for a handful and began to study it. Glancing quickly over it at first but then throwing himself into the study even more deeply than I, he began to talk, almost babble, saying, "Why there's crystals of all sorts—blues, whites, blacks, greens, beiges, reds, and pinks. My god, there is so much!" I said nothing but quietly got up and walked away. As I turned back to wave a good-bye, he was holding a bluefish in his outstretched hands, turning it in the early morning sun so that the light would splash at just the right angle for fabulous color. But I clearly saw another glistening in that rising sun. Tears ran down his face and he sobbed. I knew why too. After thirty years this was probably the first time he had ever really looked at or felt a bluefish. I think of him often, how much in life he'd missed—but also how much he'd now discovered. Every time I think of that old fisherman I think of the rush of society in general, and remember the words of Marcus Aurelius Antoninus: "it is not dying that a man should fear, but a man should fear never having lived at all."

I wonder about that old fisherman often, hoping that he had at last learned to savor, to live, life. I wonder how many people rush through life never feeling the wind in their hair or the sun in their faces, never seeing beach sands or sunsets, never hugging trees or really reaching out and touching a loved one. We all wander through life but the question is How? Do we wander like the fisherman or like Grandfather? Will we breathe in the raptures of life now or wait until it's too late?

STUDYING NATURE

Wherever mankind has left a patch of earth, even a tiny crack in a sidewalk, nature will try to fill that niche. The wonders of nature can be found anywhere we look—anyplace, city or suburb, country or wilderness—nature is everywhere. What is sad is that people think that they must travel hundreds of miles and spend a lot of money on sophisticated camping equipment to study the wonders of nature. But that's so far from the truth. Sure, there is the rapture and serenity, the pure awe and inspiration, of the wilderness, but a columbine looks just as beautiful growing in an abandoned lot as it does in any distant wilderness area. A raccoon is just as exciting prowling the pond's edge in a city park as it is near a mountain pond. Sure, we have to close off the clamor, clutter, chaos, and pollution of a city environment, but *any*place we find nature is a fascinating inspiration.

Another problem that faces the general nature-seeking public is that there are not enough wilderness areas and forest preserves to go around. Every summer people flock to the famous wild places only to find overcrowded campgrounds, lines, and masses of people. You have to be a good hiker to get away from the crowds and up into the back country, but even then your chances of being alone are slim. Unless you are like me and will visit the national parks and forests during the off seasons, even deepest winter, you will find it increasingly difficult to find solitude. Summer months will rarely find me near a national park or forest. Instead I'll spend my time roaming around my farm or in many of

Locust

the forgotten wilderness areas of the countryside, probably seeing more of nature than most of the throngs visiting our parks.

If more of us would take a long, hard look around, we would begin to see the nature that has been hidden from us for years. No matter where we live, there is always beauty to be found for those who seek it. Mysteries and adventures are everywhere. If you find yourself tired of the cities or the monotony of suburbia, there is no need to go to the grand areas of this country, to the Yosemites, the Grand Canyons, the Grand Tetons, or so many others. There are the little parks and the country settings just outside our town limits that are just waiting to be explored. Some may not have been walked in by man for decades. If we can only learn to understand the innate beauty of nature's little things, to experience the rapture of appreciation, we will truly know nature for what it is: a kind and gentle teacher that keeps us rooted to the soil even in the sterility of the largest cities.

We can all join in and begin to create havens for wildlife, no matter where we live. There should be no wasteland or garbage piles. These areas can be cleaned up by the community; trees and brush can be planted and water added at strategic locations so as to attract wildlife. We should have less finely trimmed lawns and manicured parks, and allow more brush and weedy patches to grow for the animals that would make their homes there. Whatever small thing we do for the perpetuation of wildlife, we are saving it from destruction, and enriching our lives. As you rush to your job in the morning, stop for a moment and listen to the singing of birds. Is their song any less sweet than that found in the wilderness? Take a moment and come with me into the forgotten wilderness.

INDEX

Stink gland, 45, 47
Stones, tracking over, 39
Streets, 104–6
Striped skunk, 150–53
bite, 152
breeding, 152–53
den, 153
diet, 153
life span, 152
scent spray, 151–52
stalking, 152
tracking, 191
Suburban wilderness, 11–100
tracking in, 187–89
Sumac, 27
Sunfish, 84, 128, 141, 142
bluegill, 85–87
Sunflower seeds, 124
Survival
carp as teacher of, 127–28
shelters, 116–17
Swallows, 118
bank, 141
barn, 94–96, 141
tree, 141

T

Tadpoles, 84
pickerel frog, 94
Teeth, 17, 44
Tent caterpillars, 25
Terrarium, 81
Thistle, 124
Titmice, 42
Toads, 43, 53, 168
in city, 105
Tom's River, 98, 133
Tracker, The, 4
Tracking box, 188
Tracks and tracking, 187–93
and animal signs, 192–93
ant, 38–40, 47
cat family, 189
coyote, 146
daddy longlegs, 46, 47
dog family, 189
in hedgerows, 44
how to tell, 189–92
in lawns, 17, 18
learning, 39–40, 46, 47, 48–49

medium, 39
millipede, 48–49
mouse, 18
practicing, on voles, 61, 66–67
rabbit family, 190
red squirrel's help in, 158
rodents, 190
near water, 82, 84, 142
weasel family, 190
where to find, 187–89
Trails, 49, 61, 192
Trees
fruits as bird food, 27
and tracking, 188
Tree stands, 140
Tree swallows, 141
Triungulin larvae, 50
Turkeys, 183
Turkey vultures, 138
Turtle
box, 90
observing, 141
painted, 90–91

U

Urban wilderness, 103–33
different ecological environments
in, 103
stalking and camouflage in, 195–99
tracking in, 187–89

V

Vireo, 65
white-eyed, 55–56
Virginia creeper, 27
Voles or meadow mice, 23, 61, 65,
66–68, 138–39, 146, 183
breeding habits, 68
caches, 68
cities, 61, 66, 67
in city, 109
common, 20
diet, 68
habitats, 66, 68
importance of, 61
as indicator animal, 61
tracking, 49, 61, 66
trails, widened, 72
tunnels, 61

As you know from reading this book,
sharing the wilderness with Tom Brown, Jr.,
is a unique experience. His books and his
world-famous survival schools have brought
a new vision to thousands. If you would like
to go further and discover more, please
write for more information to:

THE TRACKER

Tom Brown, Tracker, Inc.
P.O. Box 927
Waretown, N.J. 08758
(609) 242-0350

**Tracking, Nature, Wilderness
Survival School**